For M...

For

with ...

In the Heat of the Sun

ROBERT BERNEN

In the Heat of the Sun

HAMISH HAMILTON
LONDON

First pubished in Great Britain 1981
by Hamish Hamilton Ltd
Garden House 57–59 Long Acre London WC2E 9JZ

British Library Cataloguing in Publication Data

Bernen, Robert
  In the heat of the sun.
    1. France—Social life and customs—20th century
    I. Title
    944.083'092'4   DC33.7
    ISBN 0–241–10521–8

Printed in Great Britain by
Willmer Brothers Limited, Rock Ferry, Merseyside

to Derek Hill, the catalyst

Preface

The swallows at Collioure. Sitting at the old Mediterranean port. The sun is setting behind us and the moon, almost full, has risen out of the sea. The town itself is dressed against the rocks and hills that rise up to be mountains. There is still enough light for the sky to be almost blue but the first false lights are going on across the bay, rising in sequence along the contours of the hill. Opposite, on a place where the rock juts out to make the harbour, an old church stands, rough brown stone and a round bell-tower reminiscent of a tower of defence. Beyond, the green jetty-light has begun to flash. Fishing boats are moored at the quays, some of them pulled out of the water and lying on the sides of their hulls, masts stretching out diagonally, waiting to be painted.

Suddenly I become aware of the swallows everywhere above, scores of swallows moving through the sky a hundred feet above in swift, straight lines, barely swerving with little sharp cries for the insects they take on the wing. They are dark outlines against the darkening blue of the sky, their slender wings shallow crescents, their bodies slender and tapering, perfect forms for the quick, direct pursuit. They seem, above me, to be all equidistant from me, to be part of an echoing sphere of sight and sound and movement that surrounds me.

Then I notice the single gull, lower, slower, rising and falling in slow and random arcs, its body larger, its wings rising first from the body then bending away into a horizontal. Not made for swift pursuit but for an easy reconnoitering glide, the gull breaks the smooth interior surface of the sphere.

I think of the diversity of the world. The swallows are like the sphere of perception, occasionally broken by the unexpected, by the dipping gull, which breaks the simple pattern of regularity, becomes a part of myself.

Argeles Plage, Saturday, 12 May, 5 p.m. The Beach Ball. The sun still high, bright and strong. I go to the beach with my towel and bathing-suit but stop near where I have parked the car and sit in a café chair (the café is closed) under a large, shady evergreen, watching the people.

Who are mostly just sitting. Most of them old, retired. Neatly dressed. They sit on benches, hands clasped, or arms folded; or hands behind their head, or resting on the back of the bench. Waiting. Little conversation. In front of two old people a young woman sits on the pavement, talking with them, repeatedly calls her dog and tells it to lie down. The dog is restless, wanders off. She calls it back, the dog wanders on to the grass to piss. She calls it back, slaps it lightly. *Couche-toi! Couche-toi!*

Those on foot, walking, passing by, are mostly young. Lightly dressed, T-shirts, jeans, shorts, a group of young people go by, young men, a little girl in shorts with them, a young woman carrying a baby. The men have their shirts off, strong, smooth bodies. The woman wears a light red print dress, the upper part of her body curves gracefully backwards as she holds the baby in her cupped arms. Their bodies sway and rock easily in rhythm to their walking. As they walk their whole bodies are in motion, rolling forward rhythmically, participating, all the parts, in the action of walking. There are four of them but the rhythm is one rhythm for the whole group, even though they are not noticing each other, are taking each other for granted. Only the little girl is in a different rhythm, twice as fast, slightly hurried perhaps, to keep up, to be a participant.

The walking of the old is not the same, is more static. Two retired men across from me get up to go. Their bodies do not participate in the walking, they walk reluctantly, they bend the top part of their bodies forward as if starting a long journey with great effort. Their legs move, their hands are almost still. They are not, like the young, expecting something, looking forward to something, they are simply passing time. It is too late for fun, for new experience.

Look, here comes a very old man in an electric wheel chair. It hums softly as it moves him along at walking pace. Just keeping up, her hand with her purse on the back of the chair, an old woman. The chair is all fresh metal and shine, neat and orderly, with a little box under the man's right hand by which he turns and controls it. He is tall, heavy, wears a black beret, grey sweater, brown trousers, heavy black shoes, the shoes of the cripple. They go to a bench and stop. The woman sits in the middle of the bench, he parks his chair at the end of the bench, and so they sit taking the air.

A boy rides by on a bike, a smaller boy standing very erect on the luggage-rack behind him.

The young, their bodies supple; the old, their bodies stiff; the children, unconscious of themselves.

But as life proceeds this consciousness increases, grows heavier, restrains. The children, made of action, continued movement, never a pause for reflection. The young: a growing self-awareness, but in the form of confidence, expectation. The young parents yet more aware, conscious of others, evaluating, preoccupied, always aware as well of their *goal*. The old: the goal achieved, past, left now without a motive for action.

A young woman rides by on a bike, looking around. Her smoothly rounded features, her tan skin, her dark hair, black in many locks along her head.

The sun is in the west. It is no longer overhead, it is on the sides of things. It shines like a line along the sides of the trees, outlines the arms of the young women. Groups of people walk out of the sun and slowly through the shade of the broad trees, in shadow, then suddenly they are in the sun again, brightly illuminated. It is time for the swallows. The first one has appeared swooping in curves and arcs. I see the blue-black and orange tan of her plumage. Everything is conditioned by the great shade of the trees, breaking the heat and brightness of the sun. It is an oasis, a place of rest, an island through which the young and old pass between the wide areas of uninterrupted sunlight.

I go to a café for coffee. There are not many people about. I go inside, stand at the bar. A few people are sitting at the tables outside. Young men drink beer. The waiter comes in with his tray, rag and bottle-opener on it, calls for *un schweppes, un demi, un café*. He has the air of not being a waiter at all, there is something novice about him, although he is not young. It is that this is the first day, the first sunny day of the spring, the first chance to open the business and make a little money. I can feel his gladness at his first chance to make some money. The man behind the counter is the same. Inside the café, the bottles, glasses shining in rows and ranks, the brandy-snifters, the coffee machines, the heavy doors of the refrigerators, the chairs and tables, the sound of running water as the bartender washes the glasses.

When I have finished my coffee I go back to the beach and walk through the sand towards the water. There are scattered groups of bathers near the sea, sometimes two old people or two young men, two young women, a family, small children and young parents. There a woman in a long, light, loosely flowing orange dress swings her young son holding him by one hand and one foot, she swings him around and around, herself pivoting on her heels in the soft sand, his body rising and falling in arcs and circles as she wheels about. When she stops he laughs and demands more. His hair is as dark black as hers.

The younger people wear brief bathing-suits, the old people, white-haired, are fully dressed. The men roll up their sleeves, the women pull their dresses up to expose their legs to the sun. I look southward towards the Pyrenees, Collioure. The mountains rise sharply there out of the blue sea, up to the peaks where the old Spanish watch-towers of Madeloc and Massane, still there, still visible, half-ruined, keep the frontier. White breakers are rolling in from the east but a wind is blowing from behind me obliquely outwards to sea. A few hundred yards south there are fewer people, more private for a swim. I walk along, watching the sand, the sun on the rough sand, the mountains still green, still many shades of greenness in the afternoon light. I pass people playing with their children. Here a mother pretends fear of the bucket of water her little boy threatens to throw, there two little girls lie with their heads down the slope towards the sea, their legs upwards towards sky and sun. Suddenly they lift their legs and roll over head first backwards towards the water. A man with powerful shoulders is playing with his son by the side of the water. He skates a beach-ball out on the first breakers rolling in from the sea. The ball rolls back. The son retrieves it. Again the man skates it out – this time a foot too far. The wind is taking it now, blowing it outwards, away from the beach.

In a second the little boy sees what has happened. He begins to cry. 'Don't cry,' his father says quickly, 'perhaps it will come back.' *Peut-être que ça revient.* I am surprised that he doesn't plunge in after it. But the water is still cold. It is early May. He makes no move to go in. Now, already, it is too late to recover the white beach ball floating steadily further away, away and southwards, southwards towards the crags that hide Collioure. The breakers seem to become stronger, more insistent, louder, whiter, foamier.

The little boy runs to his mother, crying. The father follows, dejected, his powerful shoulders sagging, useless. He looks outward and backward, towards the lost ball. As I pass I see the three of them now, discussing, not looking towards the ball. I walk on. A small plane passes droning overhead, yellow against the blue sky. The curve of the shore. The yellow-tan sand, the blue sea, the ever-renewing changing fringe of white breakers. I pass an old man and two women, fat in one-piece bathing-suits, taking the sun. Further on a young woman lying with her head towards the sea, her uncovered breasts lying so flatly against her chest they are hardly perceived. A small group of young men and women fully clothed. I reach a less crowded place, take off my shoes, shirt and trousers. The wind is strong and I weight down my clothes with my shoes. I descend the short, sharp slope of sand that separates me from the sea, the slope of the basin the sea has cut out for itself, half-walking, half-sliding, the sand crumbling down under my feet. The sea is rough, the rolling breakers lifting the sand in curling twisting cords, a picture of its gravelly, coming-going sound, its moments of near silence only a pause to prepare new sound, new movement inward, outward. It is cold, my feet in the water feel the cold, and I move back, away.

Looking up to where I have come from I see the three, the father who skated the beach-ball unwisely too far into the water, across the waves, for the wind to take; the little boy; the mother. She is in the lead, carrying her beach-sandals, a look of dissatisfaction on her face, walking along southwards, towards the mountains, towards Collioure. The little boy follows, with the same look. Last, the father, the man with powerful shoulders, trails behind, keeps up, carrying the family goods in a bulging plastic bag, across the top of it a long French bread as yet uncut. They are walking along the firm sand by the water and he has to hold the plastic bag up high to keep the splash of the breakers from getting to the food. Same look.

Where are they going? I watch them in surprise as they file by, one after the other, the three of them, mother, son, father, disgruntled. Then I see the mother look up, stop, point to the ball. There it is! She can see it still. They are following the ball.

I see it too, having forgotten about it, but looking for it now out to sea where the mother has pointed. There it is, floating towards the distant beach southwards. It is a white dot in the distance, barely distinguishable from the white-caps except that it is smaller, tighter, whiter, floating on the surface, steadily southwards.

'There it is,' she says. They continue. I see what they are doing. They are walking towards the distant beach, to where the shore curves round and the land juts out in foothills into the sea. They are going to be there where the ball is going, to recover it.

But will they? But it is miles away, do they realize how far, how far to walk with bare feet on the sand? To me it looks as if the ball is too far out, it is not going to land on that last visible beach, that just discernible stretch of sand. It is heading for the cape, for Collioure, perhaps, around the crag, beyond it – perhaps to Spain – who knows? – perhaps beyond Spain to Africa.

A red ladybird settles on my arm as I watch them. They are walking steadily but not too fast, the mother first, with her beach-sandals in her hand, the little boy with the towel, the father last with the bulging plastic bag and the long French bread. Their look of discontent communicates itself even though I see only their backs, their walking. They stop for a consultation, look towards the ball, a tiny white dot above which the gulls wheel and swoop, rise and soar and swoop again. I watch them, the gulls, soaring and rising and gently descending, and I watch the three figures diminishing in the distance, towards the south, following the ball, heading for the distant beach. A swallow swoops and flips, its dark wings and slender split tail balancing deftly in the strong wind. The three are tiny

5

figures now moving along the fringe of wet sand between sea and beach. I can hardly see them now.

*

Les Sorbiers. The repeated soft note of the hoopoe, like a tiny owl – hoo, hoo, hoo, hoo – four notes repeated over and over again, all on the same note, the same tone. The house is new and the white stucco is fresh. There were vines on the ground before but the new owners have rooted them out, ploughed the ground fresh and put in fruit trees and asparagus. All around the little trees and tiny plants they keep the ground churned up with a small rotavator, thus discouraging the grass. The ground is yellow and dry and when the wind is strong it takes away gusts of dusty soil. When it rains the ground turns to mud, which we track in to the house on our shoes.

At dawn we hear many birds, and many different kinds. Later in the day they sing less. The heat and brightness stills them. Even at night, if there is a moon, there are some birds singing. The moon also sets the bantam rooster down the road to crowing, and the two large alsations start to howl and bark.

On a clear day Canigou, which is thirty miles away, looms up in the west, an uneven mass of snow against the sky. Today it is white but there are times when the snow is pink in the early light, and the mountain below the snow-line is so like the sky itself that the snow seems suspended in the air like some immobile, sharp, unusual cloud. Nearer to us, right beyond the house, are the hills that rise green to the south and go to the towers of Massane and Madeloc and on to the Spanish border.

*

Argeles Plage, Sunday, 13 May, a.m. – about 11 o'clock. The intense brightness of the sun throws a haze over everything: the mountains, the sea, the sand. Only the bright yellow blossoms of the broom planted along the fringe where the beach meets the pavement keep

6

their own colour under the bleaching light of the bright sun. Everything is still in spite of the strong breeze. There are only a few people on the beach, and the sea is calm. Only the very tops of the trees move restlessly. The white fronts of the red-tiled summer houses seem particularly immobile – the brightly painted shutters closed.

*

The market in Collioure. It is Sunday, but we go to Collioure to see the *sardana* – the Catalan national dance. There will be a live band, and anyone who wants to can join the dance, done with linked hands in a large circle, men and women alternating, surprisingly sedate for a folk-dance, for a national dance, the dancers hardly moving from their place, their hands always linked, the circle growing as new arrivals move in, and sometimes a second circle beginning within the first one, and other circles of dancers nearby. The quality of the dance is all in the grace and delicacy of the steps, which get slightly livelier towards the end, as the dancers jump up off the ground, rhythmically, gracefully, their hands always joined and always, throughout the entire dance, held high above their heads. The circle scarcely revolves.

I remember seeing this dance years ago in Barcelona, before the cathedral, in the open space there, and the dancers making their own music as they danced with their voices. I did not know then that it was the Catalan national dance they were doing and that it was an expression of national sentiment, of identification with something other than Spain. I thought it was a spontaneous desire to dance, an attractive remnant of spontaneity and individuality in a modern world that had done away with all that. Perhaps it was that too, but at any rate now I know that it was certainly more. It was an act of defiance to the dictatorship that, in trying to integrate Catalonia ever more tightly into Spain, wanted to discourage all expression of regional feeling. And so the dancers were having more than a good time. They were also being patriotic.

The dictator is dead now and the Catalan liberation movement is out in the open, carried on without fear. When we visited the northern part of Catalonia a few weeks ago we stumbled on to 'the

7

day of the *sardana'* in the little mountain city of Seo de Urgell, a few miles south of the frontier with Andorra. Everywhere we went we found freshly made street signs in Catalan replacing the old ones that had been in Spanish. Equally, the road signs had either been replaced or painted over by enthusiastic autonomists. The same thing was going on in France too, where Catalonia has spilled over the Pyrenees into the region the French call the Roussillon. Thus on the roads we passed signs where the names had been modified by the addition of an 'l' or an 'i', or the deletion of some letter, from a French form to a Catalan one. *Perpignan* became *Perpinyà*. All potentially confusing for the tourist, who, intent on finding his way, might think these etymological refinements irrelevant to the real problems of a country's culture and liberty.

Whether the *sardana* to be danced in Collioure today is predominantly propaganda, part of the Catalan nation's struggle for independence, or simply a joyous expression of what the dancers feel in getting together for the dance, is something we cannot decide. When we discover we will have to pay fifteen francs each to get in and watch the dance we lose interest. At any rate at eleven in the morning there is still no sign of the advertised dancing, and we wander on, stumbling by chance on the market.

The market-place is a large sandy lot with about twenty big old plane trees spread about, their leaves fresh but full now in mid-May, a large cool shade from the hot sun. It is pleasant being under them, seeing the bright light all around outside, and the sunlight in among the green leaves, the grey cool shadow.

(Cheese, olives, peppers, charcuterie, meat, clothes, herbs, pizza, records, kitchen utensils, etc.)

*

Avec préavis – 'person-to-person'. Argeles Post Office. The window where people send letters, telegrams, collect *poste restante,* cash their pension vouchers, make phone calls. I want to call Ireland 'person-to-person'. In my poor French I don't get the idea across to the young woman, but an old post-office employee nearby overhears and understands. *Avec préavis*, that is the magic phrase I was hoping for, *avec préavis* : person-to-person.

In fact, there is no need for the call to be person-to-person, I am only trying to find out whether it is possible to phone Ireland at all. For three days I have been trying to dial direct, sometimes getting as far as a busy signal, but more often collecting an odd series of noises or recorded messages. I dial one-nine, the code for out-of-the-country calls, and hear the rapid series of chirping noises the phone makes while it is searching for an open line. Sometimes those noises go on for minutes, until I hang up and start again with one-nine, and, this time, get a free line in five seconds. Then I go on to three-five-three, the *indicatif* for Ireland. Half the time I am stopped by a harsh buzzing noise after the five, but if not, if I get through the three digits without trouble, I go on to nought-one, which zeroes me in on Dublin. Then on to the number itself. Now one of several things can happen. I can get through the six digits, wait, and hear . . . silence. Silence. . . . More silence. . . . Nothing, in short. Or I can get a woman's voice in French telling me that the number I am calling is non-existent, or that it has not yet been installed, or words to that effect; or a man's voice telling me to consult the directory; or a woman's voice telling me something in German which I can't recollect or didn't understand; or sometimes I simply get a horrible noise : a harsh buzzing, a chirping again, or something else altogether.

It is all because there has been a mail strike in Ireland for three months, and a phone operators' strike as well. The only way to get through is to dial 'direct' – that is to say, any place that doesn't depend on an operator connection. For me, Dublin. But that worked, occasionally, until about two weeks ago. Now even those lines seem to have been cut. Hence the noises and recorded instructions.

The sun is so bright outside it seems sad to be sitting in the post office. The temper of the young woman who was so cheerful a few weeks ago is already wearing thin. She no longer smiles. It is only early May but the crowds of tourists are already making more work than she can handle. Crowds wait for letters sent to *poste restante,* others send packages. A man from Holland cashes his pension. Two young Germans swagger about bare to the waist, frowning, morose-looking. They remind me of our landlady's distaste for incompletely dressed Germans. 'They make themselves at home right away –

9

just like in 1940.' She doesn't mind brief bathing-suits on the beach, she is even ready to tolerate nudism (in nudist colonies, to be sure) – 'Here in France everyone is free to do what he likes, say what he likes, *bien sûr*' – but she prefers the people around her to be fully dressed when she goes shopping in the town. But this is only the beginning of the season, the merest tip of the iceberg. And the girl behind the counter will have to sit there for the four hot months to come, while the vacationers, some of them here for an entire summer of *Nichstun, dolce far niente, rien faire*, come and go in their comfortable *déshabillé*, bare feet, shorts, or bikinis, bare chests, what not. Some time or other the girl behind the counter gets three or four weeks off, perhaps during the height of the summer season when there is no getting away from the crowds, then back to the grindstone.

But in spite of all the modernity of France, this young woman seems to have all the burden of doing everything without mechanisation, by hand. In the first thirty minutes that I wait for my call she manages to handle the business of only four or five people. There is a line of eight or ten people waiting. As she works she chews her gum more and more furiously. I notice that she is writing with a ball-point pen that is chewed half to pieces at the top end; another one, also half chewed up, lies on the counter.

Finally she sends me to a phone booth – *cabine numéro deux, s'il vous plaît* – and I pick up the phone and hear the number ringing at the other end. 'No reply,' the French operator decides. At that moment an Irish voice answers. The operator explains in very clear English, but with a charmingly thick French accent, who it is I am calling. The Irish voice sounds gruff by contrast with the clarity of the French voices I have grown used to. He wants to know who is calling. I give my name. Further pause and more ringing. In the end the call does not go through, because everyone is out to lunch. I had forgotten that everything in Ireland is an hour later than here – or should I say an hour earlier? At any rate, they are still having lunch there when we have finished here.

I go back to the counter. The line has grown from eight or ten to ten or twelve. I pay the charge for the *préavis*. The world is very modern, modern technology is wonderful, but still at times it is hard to make a phone call, and the young woman behind the counter chews her gum more and more furiously while she writes numbers, names, data with her chewed up ball-point pen, and the people on the line stand patiently waiting.

*

Madame Fissier comes down in the morning to let the cat and the dog out. She is having problems with both of them. The cat, coal black with sharp yellow eyes, leapt out of a second-storey window one day when Madame Fissier was out and hurt his front paws in landing. He limps about on three legs, and she has put a leash on him and tied him up for fear he will limp off into the woods and get caught by some dog or fox. He sits or lies at the end of the line nervously twitching his black tail. From time to time he rolls over in the dust, powdering his fur.

The big alsatian bitch is a different problem. She is in heat – *en chasse* – and leaves drops of blood everywhere she goes in the house. If she is left outside the dogs might get to her, and then there will be the problem of unwanted pups. Madame Fissier has bought a 'chastity belt' for her – *ceinture de chastité* – a kind of small brown bikini with a hole for the tail. It is both to stop the dogs and also to catch the blood. It looks exactly like a modern topless bathing-suit – or rather, a grotesque travesty of one.

Madame Fissier stops at the open kitchen window to chat with my wife, who starts by thanking her for the radishes and apple tarts she left on the window-sill for us while we were out. Madame Fissier talks about the nudists at St Cyprien. She had heard about them but thought they were all Germans, who come to France for nude bathing, as well as other forms of making free of themselves. Then she heard that there were French as well among the nudists and decided they must all be Parisians. Then she heard that there were lots of local people as well – 'our sixty-sixes'. The numerical reference is to the licence-plates on the cars. Licence-plates in the extreme south-east corner of France all end in sixty-six, hence 'our sixty-sixes'. 'But,' I object, in my pidgin-French, 'if they don't wear the licence-plates – *les immatriculations* – on their chest, how do you know where they are from?' 'Ah, but you can tell from the way they speak. They have their own way of speaking, the Catalans.' It is true, it is easy to detect the Catalan accent. The reason she is surprised that even the sixty-sixes go in for nude sun-bathing and swimming is that Spaniards (and here the Catalans) have a reputation for puritanism. But here in France 'everyone is free to do as he likes, to say as he likes: it is his own business.' And then 'fashions change, bathing-suits keep getting briefer. It has become a part of the customs of the country – *il est entré dans les moeurs, n'est-ce pas?*'

*

Collioure – evening – light still in the sky but the sun has set, the colour is out of things. The waiter at the café comes over and says, *'Monsieur-Dame désirent . . . ?'* as if to take our order, but then at once puts down the little carafe of water he knows we like, the glass with the two ice cubes, and our two coffees. He has learned our habits already. Then he sits and talks, about tourism, Collioure, himself, the sea. Ten years ago, he says, there were three hundred fishermen in Collioure, a hundred fishing boats. Now there are none. Then the entire bay was filled with boats, now there are only the few we see pulled up on the quay, and those few are not for fishing but for excursions. What has happened to the fish? To be sure there is pollution, chemical pollution, as everyone knows, but also there has been plenty of overfishing. And dynamite. He describes the system by which a fishing boat sets out to sea at night and puts out smaller boats, each with a brilliant light at the bow, over the water. The light attracts the fish, which rise to the surface and are easier to catch. 'But if they are slow to rise?' – a stick of dynamite kills them all. Then they rise quick enough.

There is something ghastly in the image of the fisherman catching his already dead fish, more so in following the description of the utter destruction the dynamite works for two or three hundreds of metres around and down, killing everything, young fish, eggs, plant life, plankton – everything. Hence the gradual disappearance of the fish. Worse yet, he thinks, is the dumping of fish that can't be sold. He describes one instance : the captain who came in one morning with twelve tons of sardines and found that the market had already been saturated. He couldn't sell his fish. Instead he turned back to sea and dumped the twelve tons of dead fish. And that was only one instance. He goes on to point out the high price of tinned sardines.

He himself had come to Collioure as a tourist ten years before, had stopped to drink a cup of coffee, had been there ever since. He runs his café six months of the year to make his living, then spends the other six months painting. That way he is free to follow his artistic conscience, to paint as he likes to paint, without commercial considerations.

I thought before that he was a local fisherman who had come down to being a waiter in a café because it paid better. So far from being from Collioure he even points out, by making his hand into a tiny cup, the limited intellect of the local people. The cup illustrates the size of the brain. We do not ask him to expand on that, but it is in connection with thefts of chairs and tables from the café, or throwing them in the sea for a prank.

The port is dark tonight, for the moon is two or three nights past full and does not rise while we are there. In contrast to the past few nights, when the full or almost full moon rose from the hills across from us just at sunset and threw its warm reflection into the bay, the bay tonight and all the hills around seem very dark and the lights of the houses and the streets stand out more sharply. Everything seems more still, more silent. There are fewer people.

The waiter talks about the crowds of summer and expresses his surprise – disgust, as well – that they should choose such a crowded place for their holidays. He doesn't seem to know that every place is crowded in August. And since most people can only take their holidays in August, are only given time off in August, they have no choice, they have to go where there are crowds. There are crowds everywhere then. Solitude is a luxury of the rich, of those who are at leisure while others are working. Perhaps it is that luxury alone that puts you into the class of the rich, even if you are travelling with nothing more than a rucksack and a sleeping-bag – the luxury of being in the south of France when few other vacationers are there to compete with you for service, for space, for sun and sand and sea – for the world. Fortunately there is a compensating force : those who can never afford solitude seldom desire it. They learn to like to be where the crowds are, for it seems to them that that is where life is. Where everbody wants to be is where it is worth being, is how they feel.

I enjoy Collioure more as an outsider, before I hear its problems, its stupidities, its tedium. For I know already that, under the beautiful surface, these old fishing ports that have been transformed into pleasure places, holiday spots, have lost their quality of life and have become, at the heart, tedious – tedious to themselves.

*

Tuesday, 15 May. The *Monde* carries a little article on its back page :-

HEAVY SENTENCES FOR TAHITI PRISON MUTINY
Saturday, 12 May. The criminal court of Papeete, Tahiti, in accordance with the demands of the state prosecutor, has imposed sentence of forced labour *in perpetuity* on Mr Tauhiro, instigator of the mutiny which broke out on 14 January, 1978 in Nuutania-Tahiti prison. The mutiny resulted in the death of a guard, Edmund Pau, and a prisoner, Nadir Marsoers. Pierre Teave, Henri Chapman and Jean-Claude Temarii, who struck the guard, were sentenced to twenty years of forced labour. Joseph Siegel and Antoine Itutaouoho were each given fifteen years of forced labour, Yves Orirau twelve years of forced labour, and Felix Kapikura five years of imprisonment for criminal activities.

Sitting in the sidewalk café in front of the Hôtel de Ville in Perpignan, listening to the lively sound of young French voices, watching the people across from me, in the sun (I, for a change, have chosen the shade – the minority preference), the little cups of espresso coffee, glasses of beer, the newspapers, the smoke of cigarettes blowing away – the freedom, in short, the liberty to do as you like when you like, to drink a beer, to light a cigarette, to read a paper, I wonder what life is like in the Nuutania-Tahiti prison where eight men got fed up and killed a guard and another prisoner, for which they will recompense the state with one lifetime and eighty-seven years of hard labour divided out among the seven of them. I wonder what their lives are like day to day. I suppose they don't lack the sun-tan the rest of us are busy trying to get.

As I think these thoughts a little girl, possibly six or seven years old, her dark-toned face surrounded by thick dark curls, wearing a brown sweater and brown slacks – I have already noticed that people around here prefer these dark tonalities that match rather than compliment their own colouring – comes up to my chair and asks if I will give her a franc. *'Pourquoi tu le veux?'* I ask. *'Pour Maman,'* and then more explanation which I can't follow. I reach into my jacket pocket and, to make conversation I ask *'Quel est ton nom?'* She smiles broadly: *'Patrice.'* *'Et où est-ce chez toi?'* *'Ici, à Perpignan,'* she says. I find a half-franc coin. *'Je te donne cinquante centimes,'* I say, looking for the expression of objection that ought to come onto her face at this bit of hard bargaining. If it is there at all it is only a shadow, yielding instantly to a broad smile of enormous satisfaction at this even partial success. She takes the coin. I feel my own sense of satisfaction at having reduced the price of my alms by half, but she points at the yellow twenty centimes piece I have left on the café table for the waiter. *'Puis-je prendre ça aussi?'* *'Ça, c'est pour le garçon.'* Disappointment, then quickly she turns and runs, half skipping half jumping, around the corner, to render up the coin to *Maman*. In a minute she is back, skipping into the café, and in another minute I see her skipping out again, and hear her loud *'Merci beaucoup'* thrown back at someone. I think she must have got the full franc that time.

The young people across from me sit in the sun, wear dark glasses, smile, light another cigarette, stir the sugar in their coffee, sip their beer, read books and newspapers, improving their tans while the gentle breeze softly stirs their light summer clothing. And the boys in Nuutania-Tahiti? That's their business. Best to stay *out* of prison. It occurs to me it might have been a very narrow thing that got them in there in the first place. Maybe it all started with refusing to pay for a coffee in a café, or a beer, a fight with a waiter, arguing with a policeman. Who knows?

*

15 May. The beach at Argeles. The sun is weak, and a few thin clouds make it weaker. A brisk wind is blowing from the southeast, whipping up the white-caps and breakers on the gulf. The last two people on the beach get up to leave as I come. The yellow broom blows about restlessly back and forth in the wind. A mile

out an oil-tanker heads for Port-Vendres. Near me four wooden posts rise enigmatically out of the sand, the weathered wood yellow almost against the dark blue of the sea, the pale blue of the sky, the bleached tan of the sand.

*

15 May, p.m. – a café near the centre of Perpignan. The sun still bright and high, but a corner clock, its two faces pointing in opposite directions, tells me it is 3.15. That means 1.15 according to the sun. The young waiter cannot tell me the name of the square, so he asks the other waiter. *'Place Verdun'* is the answer, and my waiter echoes *'Place Verdun,'* and then the other again, *'Verdun,'* and so on back and forth, *'Verdun,' 'Verdun,' 'Verdun,' 'Verdun.' 'Place Verdun,'* he explains finally, *'comme la bataille.' 'La bataille,'* repeats the other. *'Comme la bataille.'* I thank them.

The great plane trees that are everywhere in the Roussillon are here too, four of them in a line along the pavement, and the same beautiful pattern of green light and shade where the leaves catch the sun. Although the square is small there are two hotels, three cafés, a few shops : clocks, shoes, clothes, what not, and on one side a huge red brick castle that is a museum now. But the major characteristic of the square is its traffic of people and cars – foot and motor. They seem to alternate, moments when the square is full of cars and trucks and motor scooters filling the little space with noise, then others when the walkers take over, quickly cross before the next wave of vehicles. The wind whips up little tornadoes of dust and dirt, a young woman walks by in a long light summer dress, her skirts pushed by the wind into restless pennants around her calves. An old man in slippers, his mouth hanging open, vacant with age, cane-supported, limps his slow way across the middle of the square ignoring the cars, letting them stop for him, their wind-screens reflecting back the sun in a sudden brilliant flash of light as they emerge from the shadow of the side-street into the open sun of the square. The dark Catalan women love to dye their hair red, but the black always remains, shines through, the result being the appearance of varnished

16

copper, metallic, harsh, unlike hair. A pregnant woman, tall and slender, straight, her belly huge and round before her, her light dress swirls around her body. Two women with small children. How the children look like the mothers! In rare intervals where cars are absent you can hear the sound of feet, the scraping of chairs, spoons against cups, human voices, talking, scolding, laughing. I think the café where I am sitting must be a great meeting place because people peer intently in as they pass, looking for someone they know.

How many silent languages are spoken here — visual expressions, cryptic communications to be interpreted by the eyes. The way each one walks, the stride, the movement of the legs, the curve of the back, the slope of shoulders, the clothes they choose, the shoes, the head and hair, the face. The young, whose bodies are no burden to them, sweep by; the old approach slowly, their progress seeming closer to stopping than to moving.

The perfect proportions of that Catalan face, unified all the more by the olive tanness of the skin, the brownness of the hair, gathered in a small tight bun at the very top and back of the skull, balancing the slight thrust of the chin. The perfect line of the lower jaw curving slightly as it moves back to join the angle of the throat. The ear is in the centre of the profiled head, a central pivotal point right where base of skull and jaw and neck join. A small gold ring hanging from the lobe of the ear is a perfect compliment to the smooth proportion of those undistorted features.

What a contrast the haggish faces and lines of the two old prostitutes who get into the car that has parked in front of where I sit. Two men with noses, lips, cheeks, chins, ears, eyes, mouths puffed and pocked with hardness, bellies round and bulging, badly dressed, get out of the car, go into the café and soon come back with the two women, their hair in disorder, one dyed red, one bleached blonde, deeply lined faces that give an impression of age although they are not old, the eyes sunk deep and — most striking of all — giving a sense of remoteness, of unease, or of long-accustomed fear.

The old man with thin white hair and the little button at his ear, the microphone on his belt, has his mouth open as if wondering whether there is something he should be hearing, his eyes wide in surprise, uncertainty. Some people impel themselves, others seem impelled, others stumble, others lag: the walk tells of certainty, uncertainty, determination, hesitation – everything.

*

The little Wednesday market at Argeles is on the Place de la Mairie – the tiny square in front of the town hall. The plane trees are still young here and do not yet give much shade, so the market vendors set up huge rectangular beach umbrellas over their stands. I sit down outside the one café, the Café de la Place, where the tables and chairs are all painted a single, determined, bright red. There is no shade but fortunately the sun is weak today. Fortunately, since even the weak sun feels hot. There are only two regular food stands at the Argeles market, one for cheese and butter and milk, the other for meat. The rest of the market is mostly long stands of sweets, bolts of material, clothing, kitchen utensils. One man has a stand entirely covered with piles of prunes, an old woman sits among boxes of garden vegetables and orange and yellow marigolds and white lilies. The ringing Catalan accent fills the square: it is like French without the clarity of French, with the singing fullness of voice of Spanish instead. There is a continual coming and going, but the pace is slow.

From where I sit at the red table I can see, through the umbrellas of the sweet vendor, beyond the cotton summer blouses and above the prunes, the mirror on the back wall of the mobile cheese shop, reflecting back from the cool shadow of the interior where it hangs the brightly illuminated bolts of cloth set out in the sun on the other corner of the square, as well as the faces of the women buying their lumps of fresh butter, cut from a single huge cube, their cheese, their yoghurt, their milk. Framing a little part of the scene as it does it turns it into a continually varying composition, a microcosm of this market morning in a French provincial town, as shoulders, torsoes, heads of old people, middle-aged, adults, children appear, pause, move across the luminous surface, and then move off. The woman who sells the cheese pushes her sunglasses back on to her bleached head, nervously combs out the ends of her short hair with her fingers, waiting for customers. Women stand in little groups and talk, arms crossed, or gesticulating by putting their open palms on their

chests. When their turn comes to talk they bend forward slightly –
a little bow. It is for emphasis, a kind of rhetoric. The children are
almost the only ones whose hair is its own colour.

In adolescence the body grows long and thin, sinuous; the adult
achieves full proportions; in old age the body contracts into itself,
shortens, becomes thicker; the old woman's mouth hangs open, a
sign of losing track.

*

The walk to Lavail. 16 May, late afternoon. We leave the house in
the still warm air and sun of the late afternoon, and follow the
road – the small back road that runs to the house and on which
there are almost never any cars – for only a hundred yards, or less,
before we turn off onto a back lane, dirt. The large alsatian at the
house there runs out as usual growling fiercely. Fortunately he is
always muzzled. *'Couche-toi – tais-toi,'* – 'lie down! be quiet!' –
we tell him, but he doesn't pay any attention to us. We walk
through the campsite at the end of the lane, a large field with many
trees and full of grass now, and no people, but in August there will
be six hundred people there every day of the month, with their
tents and cars, and probably their dogs and other pets too. The
grass is already long and the owner of the campsite has been cutting
it in sporadic swathes that seem to run anywhere, and letting it dry
before bringing it in to his barn. Apparently there is no work to
making hay here, when the weather is so dry and the sun so hot,
except the cutting and the raking up. Or does he scatter it too?

A young mare, about a year old, ambles up behind us and sniffs
our backs. She is dark brown with a black mane. A donkey, tied
by a long rope to one of the trees, looks on sadly. At the end of the
campsite we enter the woods. I look down to the right and see a
deep gorge – we are already so far out into the country – water rushing at the bottom. In another minute we come out into the courtyard of the *mas* – the word for farm here in the Roussillon – and
two large dogs rush out barking at us. But their tails are wagging.
The farm buildings are enormous by comparison with the Irish ones
we have become used to. Even the stone and brick barn and loft
is much larger than the metal haysheds of Ireland. The owner of the

mas, who is also the owner of the campsite, comes out and calls his dogs in and smiles and waves to us.

At the other end of the courtyard we come to the gorge we had been walking along, cross it on a modern bridge, looking down at the water as we go. A few yards away there is an old foot bridge, built entirely of stones in the form of a low arch, apparently without cement or any modern materials. We wonder how long it has been there.

The rest of the way up to Lavail, 1,600 feet up in the Pyrenees, is by road, with only occasional short cuts through the woods. The road crosses vineyards first with wild flowers growing along the edges, then winds through rough woodlands. We meet a flock of goats, about a hundred goats in all, feeding ravenously on all the different kinds of bush and brush. Their neat forms and sleek hair attract us and we stop to watch them. One of them, a black one with high curving horns, rises up on her hind legs, as if she were going to stand on them, but then, after an instant's balancing, leans forward against a tall thin tree, puts out her right foreleg and catches a high branch with her hoof, bending it down with her as she descends again towards earth. Quickly she starts to eat the fresh, untouched leaves of the branch, perched as she is diagonally against the tree. She has not entirely solved the problem even then, how-ever, for the best leaves are not the ones in towards the trunk of the tree and the base of the branch but those out towards the end, and she is resting against the trunk. If she tries to move outwards she will fall and the branch will slide up again. So she has to twist her long supple neck around behind her to get the leaves she wants and stretch her wide mouth outwards towards them. There are also the other goats to reckon with, for some of the less supple ones, and especially the smaller, younger year-old goats, stay near the black goat and rush over when they see that she has bent down a branch and begin furiously tearing at the outer leaves. In any event she does not seem to pay any attention to this competition but goes on eating the leaves within her reach until suddenly, and surprisingly to us, she reaches her right foreleg up again and pulls down another branch, and begins eating those leaves. I say surprisingly, because we had thought she had reached the highest branch she could. Instead, she catches still another branch when she has finished with the second.

And when she has finished with that one too she slides down back to the ground, letting the branches slip up under her leg. As she moves on to the next tree we notice she is limping and using her right foreleg gingerly, and we wonder if it is sore from the friction of the branches escaping upward along it. As the goats move along from bush to bush and tree to tree their copper bells ring hollowly on many different tones. It is the characteristic sound of the herds and flocks of the Pyrenees and further on we will hear the continual soft tolling of larger, deeper-sounding bells on the cattle that graze among the trees and on the high upland pastures. When some of the goats begin to wander too far away from the others the shepherd calls to his brown dog and the dog rushes out and herds the wayward goats instantly back into the flock, working without a sound, running beyond them and looking at them to let them know where he wants them to go.

The shepherd, who has been sitting on the grass below the road while his goats graze all around him, comes up to the road and waves to us. He tells us, in words we only understand with difficulty (no doubt he is speaking Catalan and not French) that one of the goats is about to give birth to a kid, and he leads us to where she is, lying apart from the others, not grazing, simply waiting, in a quiet grove below the road, almost completely hidden by the bush and brush and trees. For a moment we look at her, her huge flanks extended on either side of her resting form, but when we see her stop chewing her cud and begin to look curiously at us, slightly uneasy, we realize that she does not welcome the presence of strangers. If we keep looking she will get up in a moment and move off, so we quickly turn and continue upwards along the road.

A detour into the woods takes us along a dirt lane to an abandoned monastery and monastery church. Not far off are the crumbling walls of an old *mas*. The old vines of the farm are still there, but the grass has grown up all around them and they have not been pruned and they will not produce any grapes. Someone from Paris has bought the land and is going to fix it up as a holiday home, or else is just keeping it as an investment.

We rejoin the road a few hundred yards further up and follow its winding across the river again and then into narrow curves where only one car at a time can pass. We stop to watch a man earthing up his potatoes with a tool we have never seen before, a kind of cross between a hoe and a fork, a broad hoe with three thick, interjoining tines. The earth is crumbly and the work looks as if it should not be too hard, but he pauses, rests his hoe-fork against the ground, takes off his cap and indicates to us with a gesture that he is sweating. The weather is hot, even in the late afternoon and at a thousand feet, for that kind of work.

We walk on and pass a small herd of black and white mountain cattle with one or two bulls among them, their long horns curving forward on their foreheads, their long hair hanging along their sides. They watch us curiously as we pass. We stop to watch a bird perched on a wire, singing. We can see his beak parted as he utters a single repeated note over and over again before starting a series of rapid gymnastic chirpings, varying rapidly from one musical ornament to another. The woods are full of the different sounds of birds answering one another. Ahead of us now we see the *Tour de la Massane* — the tower of Massane — another two thousand feet higher into the mountains. It stands on a rough peak of rock that juts out even higher than the surrounding ground, a perfect round tower, with no other building around it. The chronology of the tower is uncertain. There seems to be no doubt that it was set up as a watch-tower, but there is a difference of opinion as to whether the occasion was the Arab invasion of Europe or some treaty between the French and the Spanish many centuries later. In the first case the tower would be more than a thousand years old, in the second only a few hundred. In any event, it has been there long enough to have become a monument. Since it has none of the elements of a castle, or fortification, it can only have been a watch-tower, and in fact there are a whole series of watch-towers along the crests of the mountains. At any sign of invaders fires would be lit, and the alarm given and passed along in that way. There is another tower visible from where we are staying, further over towards the Mediterranean, the *Tour de Madeloc*, above Collioure. It is the easternmost of the Pyrenees towers.

Although the road is all upward it has only taken us forty-five minutes of walking to reach Lavail. We have brought along a basket of food for an evening picnic and sit down at one of the tables under the trees. This time they are not plane trees but lindens, and the old lady who has come out to greet us explains to Satia that they are just coming into bloom and that when the flowers appear she will gather them and dry them – gather them in the early morning, no other time of day, she emphasizes, and dry them inside a shed in a cool, shady place, never in the heat of the sun – and save them then to make a kind of medicinal tea with. The old lady is full of such lore and loves to share her knowledge with my wife, who is an attentive listener. In the five or six times we have gone to Lavail dozens of recipes have changed hands that way, the old lady punctuating her rapid descriptions of her particular way of preparing some food or herb with smiles of approval for what she considers the right way, frowns of distaste for incorrect procedures she is careful to warn us against. As she comes to the end of each recipe, and the prepared dish is verbally imagined to be ready for serving, a satisfied smile comes to her face and she wipes her hands softly one across the other in an eloquent gesture of work well done : now everyone can go ahead and eat, it seems to say.

A similar gesture of wiping her hands accompanies the quick, hasty description of the wrong ways that people can fall into following the same recipe – hasty, fleeting, because, you sense, even though it is touched on only in words, no one wants to dwell on such wrong practices for long. This time, when she wipes her hands, she is wiping them of whatever it is she does not approve of, and the little frown enforces the sense. And we assent enthusiastically, for her peasant good sense always seems to be ahead of the careless practices of the modern world. She, like so many backward farmers we have known in Ireland, distrusts just those things the rest of us will come to disapprove of only after scientists have given us ample proof of their dangerous qualities. Thus we find it easy to talk to her. She likes her food pure. She values the milk of her own herd, grazing high in the mountain slopes and pastures of the Pyrenees, where the air and rain is still pure and the milk is healthy. She would never drink any milk from the town for she knows – she deduces – that it must contain preservatives, or else it could not be kept for so long. A little thought about the dates stamped on the milk cartons we buy makes it clear that she must be right. The frown of distaste and contempt that passes so quickly across her face makes the adulterated taste come to my mouth. On the other hand *we – nous autres* is the term she uses, 'we others' – drink nothing but our own milk, pure from the clean mountain, from animals we know. She stops for an instant and listens for the deep soft sound of one of the large copper bells, then, smiling, she gestures towards the sound. 'Do you hear?' she asks, with a broad smile — *les vaches* — 'the cows.'

When she hears we have been in swimming down at the beach, and I mention my doubts about the purity of the Mediterranean, she begins to praise the water of the river that flows down out of the mountains and gathers into a deep pool not far from where we are talking. She tells us we can swim there in perfect safety, the water is clean, there are no chemicals in it. It is the same with the fish. She will never buy the fish from the Mediterranean. Everyone knows about the pollution of the sea — the little frown flashes fleetingly across her face — and the chemicals, and the sewerage that is pouring into it constantly. If she eats fish at all she eats the fresh-water fish from the mountain streams. But, after all, she is not that fond of fish, nor of meat. 'Give me a good potato,' she concludes, once more with a smile of satisfaction. 'It is nicer than any meat — light, digestible.' Another reminder of the farmers of Ireland.

We admire the rose-bushes that surround the little pebbled terrace we are sitting on and she points out one in particular, a pink rose that is just coming into bloom, although the others are already heavy with blossoms, exactly as they are in the middle of the summer back in New York, or late summer in Ireland. The pink one, the one she is showing us, was planted by her grandmother, she says. Then, as she goes off for the wine we have ordered to go with our picnic, we speculate on just how old that would make the original shoot. The old lady herself is seventy-two, we know that because she has told us. How old would that have made her mother? Was she born a hundred years ago? And the grandmother? A hundred and thirty? Or longer? In any event the original shoot of the pink rose goes well back into the nineteenth century, and that sets our minds to speculating on what Lavail was like then. Surprisingly little was different, perhaps, although now there is a modern road to serve the dozen houses of the hamlet, and the light wires bring electricity. All to the good. What is regrettable is the depopulation. The old lady can remember when the slopes were full of herds of goats. Now there is no one to herd them, so there are no more goats. The heather and brush has grown out to the point where it would no longer be good grazing even if the goats were brought back. And she points out how many people are out of work, but no one willing to do the kind of work that could be done up here. So all this potentiality is lost, all that healthy goat-milk and goat-cheese.

Although she is in her seventies she still moves with the rapid movements, talks with the rapid voice of youth. As she talks I admire her Catalan features, see under the lined and sunken contours of her face the young Catalan face I see around me so often in Argeles and Perpignan, the perfect arc of forehead, the long, slender nose, the slightly pointed, perfectly balanced chin, the long line of her jaw, balancing and underlining the roundness of the head. In spite of the deep wrinkles there is something smooth yet and fine about the skin. Her eyes are full of liveliness.

As we begin to eat four small cats come around and wait for food at our feet. I throw down the rind of a bit of sausage but the black cat I have dropped it in front of does not see it. A grey cat, part white part black, dashes in in an instant and snatches up the morsel. Then she looks up at me and softly miaows a request for more. The voice is almost inaudible but the request is clearly written on her face. She seems more alert than the other cats. The old lady explains that her son likes the black and white one and feeds it as he eats. The black ones wandered around from some other house when they were kittens and no one could be bothered to kill them, so they have remained. Clearly there is not enough extra food to keep all these cats alive, and I can guess that most of them will not last out the year. They are in some sort of a daze that makes them slow to find the food I drop in front of them. But when I cut a small piece of Swiss cheese and drop it near the black and white cat she raises her two front paws with a swift gesture and catches the cheese in mid-air, clasping it tightly between her paws. When she has eaten it she turns her head upwards again towards me, asking for more, licking her lips with a special appreciation that lets me see she is aware of the quality of the cheese. Seeing the cats, a brown sheep dog comes over and stands near to us, not begging, just standing, waiting patiently for his share. The old lady runs over with a long, flexible rod and chases the dog and cats away, good naturedly, not touching them, just threatening. Apart from the sound of our eating and our talk, the singing of the birds, the distant cow-bells, the mountain stream, there is no other sound, no machine noise. The old lady sees the thought on our faces. 'Yes,' she says, 'we are well off here.'

We look up towards the mountains, the tower, the grey rock that rises out of the deep green of the bush, the fresh green of the leafy trees just putting out their new leaf now in the warm spring. It is an hour and a half on foot to the tower. Beyond the tower lie high mountain meadows, surprisingly green and flat. Another hour's walk and you are at the Spanish frontier.

*

16 May. The *Monde* carries another article on the back page on the Tahiti mutiny trial :-

PAPEETE MUTINY TRIAL BRINGS TO LIGHT
PRISON CONDITIONS IN TAHITI.

This time the article is longer, and raises some questions. 'Was the mutiny an act of personal resentment against the prison governor?' the *Monde* asks. 'Or was it mass insanity, or was it the first step towards a broader political movement aiming at the ultimate independence of Polynesia? . . . According to the testimony of prisoners who were not involved in the mutiny, the mutineers' aim was to seize the prison, take hostages, hold out for the independence of their country (and for a stop to nuclear tests).' Then there is a brief discussion of bad prison conditions, drinking among the guards, etc. The conspirators were all between the ages of eighteen and twenty and were all serving terms of only a few months. 'Conditions were anarchic,' the article concludes.

So, that suggests the answers to some of the questions. And if they serve out their sentences one will finish his life in the French jail, however long he lives, most of the others will be in their thirties or forties when they are released. But what chance of going fifteen or twenty years without getting into more trouble – more years, possibly life, at forced labour – *travaux forcés*?

*

Satia beginning to read *Le Tour de la France par deux Enfants*, horrified by what she reads. She points out that under the pretentious guise of realism the book is really sentimental and false. 'No wonder young people revolt,' she says, 'when their text-books give such a false picture of the world.'

The book is a text-book for schools first published a hundred years ago. It was republished recently to mark the centenary. It starts with two orphan brothers, eight and thirteen years old, trying to escape from German-occupied Alsace-Lorraine in 1871. A family friend sends them to a mountain guide who can lead them secretly across the Jura mountains by night and in to Free France. But when they get to the guide's farm they find him laid up with a broken leg, unable to go anywhere. Is that to be the end of their patriotic resolution to return to their native country?

The older brother decides to study a map of the region he finds hanging on the wall, and after a few hours of briefing by the guide himself he and his younger brother set out at nightfall to cross the mountains. They each have a stick, a bundle of clothes, and a box of matches. The mist descends and they can see nothing. But they must be across the frontier by dawn, or else the German border guards will find them. In spite of darkness, mist, fatigue and weakness, they find their way to France before it gets light.

In reality, of course, it is far more likely that they would have wandered about in circles in the darkness and mist until the Germans found them in the morning. The crossing into France is only the beginning of a long trip in search of a lost uncle, in the course of which they work their way through almost all of France, fall ill, recover, are shipwrecked and miraculously saved, and so on, until they finish up safe and sound and increasingly prosperous on a neat, orderly, well-managed farm of their own right in the middle of France. Never once, in the course of three hundred and eighteen tightly printed pages, does a witticism pass their lips.

*

Collioure. The port. A sweep of rock out into the sea enclosing a bit of it into a port. If the water is always in movement at the beach at Argeles, here it is usually still. At the ends of the distant capes, beyond Port-Vendres, there are breakers from time to time, but seldom here. The hills are green and brown, brown where the road has cut a path through or where the ground has been levelled to make building sites for houses, green everywhere else. On the slopes behind the town steep vineyards rise up towards the crests. At the very top is an ancient fort.

Another fort juts out into the port itself, dominating the port seascape with its severe lines. It is built of the same rubble-and-fill construction as the local houses and its walls have a dull brown, irregular, patchy look, but time has also given it a patina and a kind of unity. There are even two trees that someone planted in the meagre flat spaces left in front of the severe walls. All in all it is so much better than most of the pink and peach stucco of the modern houses that it does not seem like an eyesore.

Three hundred yards further out – the very last thing in town – stands the church, a plain, rectangular building that you would not notice except for its unusual round tower, built right out in the sea itself, and attached to the body of the church by a series of inter-mediate wings. The tower's bells, which have a beautiful soft ring, hang in bays near the top. The round, mound-like roof is pink.

Tonight, sitting drinking coffee and admiring the church, we notice a kind of porch of red brick built right along the side of the church and facing out onto the port, resting on a series of little supports built into the wall below it. It is perched about fifteen yards above the level of the water, and twelve or fifteen vertical slit-like windows – the kind that allowed medieval archers to shoot at their attackers without being shot at – give the appearance of a castle wall. Hence we conclude that it originally had some sort of defensive purpose. On a closer approach we discover that it is, in fact, the public toilet – the W.C. – and that the narrow windows are there to admit a little light and ventilation. Its position, perched as it is over the sea, permits the town to dispense with plumbing and sewer-age, as it flushes right into the water. I suppose it was built on to the church because there was no other convenient position for it or else because that was where it was most wanted. In any event, since all sewers in Collioure empty into the sea, it makes sense to locate the public W.C. where it is.

*

Posters on the walls at Elne : -

Pour précipiter le saccage de notre
agriculture, 9 ministres de la CEE
à Perpignan –
Le Roussillon veut vivre.
Relevons le défi . . .
Manifestons lundi 14 mai à 18h30
Place Arago, Perpignan

To hasten the devastation of our
agriculture, 9 ministers of the EEC
at Perpignan –
The Roussillon wants to stay alive.
Let us defy them . . .
Demonstration Monday, 14 May, 6.30 p.m.
Place Arago, Perpignan.

Nous n'arracherons plus un pied de vigne!
(Picture of a hill-side vineyard)
Non à l'entrée de l'Espagne, du Portugal,
de la Grèce
dans le Marché commun.
Parti communiste française.

We will not root out another vine!
NO to the entry of Spain, Portugal
and Greece
into the Common Market.
French Communist Party.

Nous n'arracherons pas nos arbres fruitiers!
(Picture of fruit orchard)
Non à l'entrée de l'Espagne, du Portugal,
de la Grèce
dans le Marché Commun.
Parti communiste française.

We will not uproot our fruit trees!
NO to the entry of Spain, Portugal
and Greece
into the Common Market.
French Communist Party.

*

18 May, p.m. Collioure. The young soldiers from the fort are training in the port. They are paddling around on their black life-rafts, their orange life-jackets making a bright, orderly pattern against the luminous blue of the sea. Buzzing around them in large grey rafts equipped with heavy, khaki-painted outboard motors are instructors in bright red tights and tops. In the cafés all the chairs face the sea, occupied by a fascinated audience.

The soldiers, seven to a raft, six to paddle and one to steer, paddle their rafts to the gravelly beach right in front of the cafés. Under the barked instructions of the instructors they jump out into the sea and carry their rafts on to the shore. The rafts are inflatable, two long cigar-like pontoons that curve around to meet in front with some kind of low deck between them to make the bottom of the raft. Ropes and hand-grips run along the outsides of the pontoons, but there are no seats or cross benches. The rowers sit on the long pontoons instead, three to each pontoon, with their feet inside, and propel the raft with short wooden paddles. A seventh man sits at the back and directs the raft by using his paddle as a rudder. It seems as if they have not had much practice at paddling since the paddles rise and fall irregularly and the rafts make uneven progress.

Once on shore they stand around their rafts – there are four groups of them – while the red instructors deliver lectures in clear, determined, unambiguous voices. The soldiers all have their hair cut very close to the head, neat in contrast to the shaggy disorder of all the young men in the cafés. They concentrate on their training: I don't see any of them looking around as if distracted. They are unaware of the people sitting at their ease, drinking coffee and beer and pernod and looking on. They are almost as intent as their instructors, who are themselves only a few years older than they are.

The instructors show them how to capsize their rafts by sitting, all together, on one of the pontoons, holding on to the hand-grips of the opposite pontoon, and then leaning backwards. The first raft is capsized that way onto the beach, the soldiers tumbling lightly backward almost as if in formation. Two instructors with paddles climb on to the capsized raft, carefully demonstrating the way to avoid putting weight on the flimsy deck between the two pontoons, spreading their legs instead and straddling the raft by walking awkwardly along the pontoons, one foot on each pontoon. They insert their paddles into the ropes on the pontoon to the left, transfer themselves to the pontoon on the right, take a firm hold on the tops of the paddles and lean back in unison, with a kind of rhythm and harmony that shows how many times they have done this. Their weight on the paddles pulls up the pontoon on the left, and as they step lightly back on to the sand the raft rights itself.

The soldiers launch their rafts and we expect to see them go through the same exercise in the water but instead they simply paddle out towards the open sea. The instructors in the grey rafts buzz about them officiously. After a while they round the jetty further in towards the town and disappear.

At the café next to ours a young light-peach-coloured cat has taken advantage of the distraction to crawl into one of the empty café chairs facing away from the port and curl up on the bright orange cushion for a snooze. She stretches herself and licks the fur around her whiskers, puts her head down and closes her eyes.

Now another group of soldiers has appeared. They are also wearing the orange life-jackets of the first group but their fatigue uniforms are blue instead of khaki. Instead of rafts they are equipped with little khaki-coloured two-man canoes. There are about twelve or fifteen of them and after a certain amount of instruction they launch the canoes into the water, climb in and paddle away. Their paddles have two blades, one at each end, and they are learning to dip the ends alternately into the water and thus paddle in unison. There is also a little rudder at the end of the canoe, which must be worked by their feet, since neither of the two paddlers has a hand free. At first they paddle awkwardly, clapping paddles against each other, going in crooked lines, making little progress, but soon they get into harmony, left, right, left, right, left, right, moving directly out towards the open sea. The grey outboard rafts buzz loudly around them back and forth, throwing up rough wakes to impede their course. Gradually, in irregular courses, the little group makes its way towards the sea, diminishing in size as they move away from us, the orange life-jackets and yellow paddles making ever-changing patterns against the blue sea as the canoes move into denser or more open groupings, constantly shifting the formless formation of their movement, rising and falling at irregular intervals on the gentle swell of the sea. Around them always the buzzing grey rafts each with its single red occupant. There is something bizarre about the scene. The little canoes with the constantly rising and falling paddles and the orange-bodied figures with neat dark heads, two to each canoe, are reminiscent of so many water insects with rising and falling legs and brightly coloured bodies and black heads moving somewhere, in some general direction, by fits and starts, with false turns, with incomplete searchings. The noise of the buzzing outboards reinforces that strange impression, as if the buzzing were coming from the paddlers and not from the supervisors. Oddly enough there is also something in the scene that reminds us of a medieval painting, some episode from the life of some saint, perhaps, neither of us can quite think what. The association is too inappropriate. Or appropriate, perhaps, since the soldiers are exercising entirely without machinery, have gone back to a time when men did everything by hand, by their own power. But gradually, as they pass the outer jetty of the port and turn to move off behind the light that flashes its green warning after dark they achieve the formation of a perfect single file, and that is the last we see of them, paddling away beyond the jetty and the church, the grey rafts following them.

Now a large grey motor launch appears surging officiously out into the bay, its prow rising and plunging against the water. Four or five of the men in red stand about on the gunwales, and we can see the black rafts loaded on the roof of the launch. But where are the soldiers? Then we see them, their orange life-jackets just visible, seated in neat ranks. Another exercise is beginning. The launch stops and the soldiers clamber in groups each to their own raft. One by one they launch their rafts from the back of the launch into the water, climb in, paddle off, return, climb on to the launch, pull the raft up again. The exercise repeated. Already we can see them growing more adept, more supple in their use of the raft, in their comings and goings on the water, between raft and launch. Now they go on to a new exercise. The launch roars out to sea, then turns and speeds back into the port. Suddenly a red instructor gives the shouted command and two groups of soldiers drop their rafts into the water and jump after them from the speeding launch, a shout of hurrah rising from them as they do so. They swim after the rafts, climb aboard, paddle about, return to the launch. And the same again. Finally they move away from the launch, paddle towards shore, capsize their rafts, right them, climb into them and paddle away at last towards the fort.

The spectacle over, the audience gets up to leave. The cafés are mostly deserted now, it is dinner time, and only a few of us stay on watching the light on the sea, admiring the green and yellow-brown of the opposite hills, the setting sun throwing a dim light on to the distant many-faceted fortress, the vineyards climbing the slopes. A young boxer dog comes around, his short fur clean and gleaming with good feeding and good care, his tail neatly clipped, his black balls hanging tightly between his legs. He holds his head high and only sniffs things at his own level, as if disdaining to put his nose down and sniff the ground. Saliva dribbles from his pugnacious jaw. He sniffs my shoe, which I have crossed over onto my knee, but even as he sniffs he does not look at it, looking away instead, sniffing perfunctorily. He is like some officious bureaucrat looking for something out of place to put right. The next moment he detects the cat snoozing in the neighbouring café. In an instant he is there, poking his nose at the cat. But the snoozing cat is already awake, reared back into a tight arch, one paw lifted menacingly, tearing the air an inch from the boxer's nose with her claws, her jaws wide, hissing fiercely. The dog stands just beyond reach of the claw, barking loudly. To me it sounds like a bark without meaning, without intelligence, the bark of the petty official. The cat hisses and shows its claws. The dog barks, then stops. A brief intermission, during which the dog looks around, as if distracted, the cat withdraws its claws, closes its mouth, its fear obvious. If its fear becomes too great it will not be able to defend itself against the dog, it is only its courage that is protecting it. Again the dog starts to bark, again the cat hisses and claws the air before the dog's nose. The dog retreats slightly, advances again, barks. Then he stops, looks around officiously, looking for something else that needs his attention, ambles off. The cat pauses for a moment and then jumps down from the chair and runs off through the little round café tables, its long furry tail flying behind it.

We look up. The canoes have reappeared, returning from where-ever it was they went to. The sensation of water-bugs again as they come into sight accompanied by the buzzing of the grey rafts. They paddle around the jetty and disappear. The exercises are over for the day.

We too get up to go, pausing on our way back to the parking lot to notice the displayed canvasses of the local artists : luscious sea-scapes with elegant white boats under sail in warm and glowing colours against the rich blue of the sea, luminous bathers in almost invisible bathing suits catching a tropical sun on golden sands, fairy landscapes of sea, sand, towns and mountains, all the opulent varieties of imagination working itself out in oils, water-colours, pastels, strange transformations of the vacation reality of the place. Just around the corner we come on the soldiers beaching their rafts and canoes just within the fort walls, discussing the day's exercises.

*

Collioure, Saturday, p.m. There is a chilly mist over the town and bay as we come around the mountain bend and look down on the port. The weather has changed completely from what it was. Walk-ing along towards the waterfront we consider changing cafés for once, going to an indoor café and having a glass of wine instead of the usual coffee. But I find it hard to abandon a habit.

In any event, the owner of our café had the same idea, for we find his doors locked, the orange cushions taken up, the wicker seats deserted. The port is sombre with mist, the light cold and damp. The castle on the hill is just visible, little more than a dim silhouette, the very top of its round tower disappearing in the cloud. The hill below it is an obscure shape, the vineyards barely distinguish-able, and the waterfront houses and buildings are under a veil. This is what Collioure must look like in winter – misty, wet. The sea is rough this evening for the first time since we have been here, and the breakers roll in and smash against the base of the jetty-light throwing up brief irregular mounds of white spray, falling back, continuing inward to break again against the tower of the church and whitely along the base of the church wall and roll at last on to the pebbly beach, the soughing sound of the rolling breakers repeated again and again every few seconds – it seems very often. A lonely tourist walks out to the very end of the inner jetty, then back again. The three portside cafés are empty except for one young woman who sits doing a water-colour. Tourists wrapped in raincoats and anoraks wander by. The swallows shriek as they wheel back and forth catching the evening insects. A young couple walk their dog along the beach. The sound of the sea, its continually rough coming and going, dominates everything. That, and the mist. Even the lights across the bay seem cold.

*

A tall glass full of wild flowers. There are five kinds of flowers, a deep yellow, a pale yellow, a purple, a red, a white. There are six of the deep yellow, two of the pale yellow, three of the red, one of the purple, two of the white, all surrounded and mixed with a lot of green leaves of different kinds.

The deep yellow flowers have the rich bright yellow of the yoke of a farm egg, there is orange in that yellow, even though I only see it as yellow. There is even red in the yellow, somewhere, but I do not see the orange and the red, I only see the yellow, deep, intense, bright, pure, like the yoke of a good egg, a bit of the yoke left on a white plate. I count the petals of one of the yellow flowers, there are eighteen, and they grow in little overlapping series, one overlapping the other in a little flat spiralling succession upwards, until finally the top is reached and they go down and start again, a little more than half an inch long, ending in two gentle points, like the rounded points of a dessert-spoon, with lines and creases running their length – the length of the petals – so that the light that falls on them only catches the tops of the surface of each petal, and I see the yellow more intently for the lines and creases of shade. It makes for two yellows, the yellow that is all light, and the yellow that is mixed with the blackness of shade. And in the centre, surrounded by all the radiating petals that come from it, a countless small mass of tiny dots, tiny yellow dots, too many to count and yet each distinct, visible in the play of light and shade. Yellow of the same yellow as the petals that spread out from them, but different in the feeling they present to the eye, because made up of so many tiny parts, a grain of light and shade.

Some of the yellow flowers lean over towards me and some lean away, a middle one is just in profile, and on it the delineating areas of light or shade become more like lines than like areas. I see the profile of the deep yellow wild flower, I notice the thin green stalk leading down to the glass, into the water. The ones that lean away are patterns of transparency, the light shines through the petals instead of coming back to me off the top of them, and the layers of transparent petals make patterns of deeper and thinner shadow, duller and brighter colour.

A fly is busy on top of one of the flowers. I observe the perfect black of his head and chest, the gleaming blue-black of his body, the intense black and gentle curve of the fine line of his legs delicately splayed and flexed to take his small weight and spread it out lightly on the flower. His wings, which I see from the side, are like lines of light. He has a long nose, like an elephant, which he pokes into the dots in the centre of the yellow flower. It is a long extension with a flat plate at the end – all black, all a pure, clean black – and he pokes the black plate on to one tiny yellow nodule after another. It is like the trunk of an elephant, except that it is jointed, and more busy. He flies to another yellow flower, now back to the first one, the one he was on before. He stays on that one for a long while, then off to another, but then again back to the first. He has a preference for that one.

I pick up my magnifying glass. He is so busy he does not notice me looking at him. The yellow light of the flower bounces back on to his blue-black belly and mixes with it, it becomes blue-black-yellow. I see the short rough hairs on his legs, the hairs jutting out of his back, the little flattened head – oval in the side view – busily bent to its work, and the yellow grains of pollen from the flower caught on the rough hairs of the front legs. He is busily rubbing his legs. Now he sees me, he stops, suspicious, he flies away. I hear him buzzing around, annoyed perhaps. He is back now on another flower and I put up the magnifier. His legs are perfectly clean now, he has brushed off the pollen, possibly he has eaten it. Was that what he was busy eating? Pollen? Like a bee? Now he is suspicious. He stands very still as I watch him, watching me, I imagine, in return, through the magnifying glass. He flies away.

36

The pale yellow flowers are different. They have many narrow straight petals like flattened straws, too many to count, coming out in a great bunch from the centre, not in a single flat plane, and at the very tip, on the little narrow edge at the very end of the petal, there is a touch of purple, like the colour on the outside edges of the pages of a book, this little touch of purple on the end of the petals of the pale yellow flower. And the yellow is a cool yellow, there is no orange on it anywhere, possibly there is a sense of the cool tones of a lake, the sea, deep down where the sun is filtered by many yards of water; there is the suggestion of straw, of paleness, coolness, retreat, so much so that the difference of light and shade are less important, and the pale yellow flower seems simpler than the bright yellow one, less complicated, even though there are hundreds more petals. And in the centre, when I raise my eyes to look, a small black clump of the tiny grains, tiny particles, very black and intense.

The red flowers hang in large floppy petals, only a few petals to a flower, like a lady's summer hat, textures of crepe, loose hanging transparencies of light red and darker red as the light passes through the thin texture of the floppy red petal. Inside it is like a garden of long dark stalks ending in little black beans, the black beans themselves divided into two little parts, like two tiny loaves attached along their whole length.

There is a bug on the red flower too, crawling along, waving and waggling his two tiny antennae, not like the fly but longer, thinner, flatter, his gleaming dark wings folded completely down on to his back, on to his long low body as he crawls tentatively about on the flower, his legs curving outwards sideways from him. He is shy and crawls out of sight, but I find another one on one of the deep yellow flowers. He is crawling slowly, searching in the tiny yellow grains just as the fly had done. But instead of a proboscis, an elephant's trunk, he has only two claw-like pincers coming out of his jaws, and he puts his whole head down to search and eat in the flower, like a dog sniffing the ground, eating his meat, like a sheep grazing. Looking at him sideways-on, I see the three black legs that are on the side near me.

The purple flowers are small, very small, and hang down in tiny separate entities along the fine green stalks that branch off from the central stalk that is in the water in the glass. The little flowers hang down in rows from the stalk, delicate membranes like purple fly's wings, veined, diaphanous, the largest ones nearest the base of the stalk, the smallest ones out towards the end of the stalk, less developed, the ones at the very end still sheathed in a green covering. On other thin stalks there are only the very beginnings of these flowers, only the palest suggestion of lilac at the part nearest the base, all the rest tiny green pods, waiting to grow, to open. And on other stalks only a tight mass of clustered points, the very beginning of the development of the pods. And on other stalks, the leaves, long, oval, the green colour of peas, arranged in perfect ranks following one another along, slightly larger towards the base of the stalk, slightly smaller further out, diminishing perfectly from stalk to tip, and beyond the stalk curling and twisting around in tiny tendrils.

The white flowers are like bells, little bells splaying out, eight or ten of them, from the very centre of the very end of the stalk, splaying out and bending over to hang sideways, downwards, some of them closed still like elongated drops of opaque white liquid, liquid sugar, others opened out into irregular, flanged bells, six small, elongated pointed petals curving in arcs outward, a fine green vein drawn along the central line of each arc, each petal. And in the centre of each bell, at the end of a small cluster of fine light green stalks, a little group of yellow dots.

*

Sunday, 20 May. After several days of haze and threatening clouds and indecisive storms it finally poured rain last night, and this morning the sky is clear again, the air cool and the sun bright. After the rain the sandy market square of Collioure is moist underfoot, almost muddy in places, but the market is none the less lively. It has the busy quality of a rural fair. Satia thinks it the best market anywhere around and it is easy to see why : plenty of stands, plenty of vendors, vegetables, fruit, cheese, meat, olives, nuts, sausages, *patés*, eggs, clothes and kitchen utensils, an endless variety of good things for the home, for domesticity, for cooking and eating and enjoying. Passing a vegetable stand I see three different kinds of lettuce, boxes of artichokes, celery, spring onions, beans, new potatoes, large dark onions, bananas, apples, pineapples, figs, dates, raisins, nuts, and so on, and on, twenty varieties of olives, peppers, chains of sausages, terrines of *paté* – *paté de campagne, paté de canard, paté de oie,* etc., etc. – cheeses: *cantal, comté, hollande, tomme, St André, chèvre, fromage des chaumes,* etc., etc., fifty kinds of cheese, and finally the pizza stand, the little white Renault van, the size of a camping van or smaller, with the black lettering along the side : PIZZA, the same in green along its forehead : PIZZA, and a big illuminated (or illuminable, at night, but not on now) glass sign : PIZZA on four metal legs on the roof; and the back and sides folding out into a counter to sell the pizza from. Inside, bending over, visible only from the waist to the shoulders, the pizza-man's thin wife, busily making the pizzas and sliding them into the searing hot oven, sliding them out again – bubbling with heat, steaming – wrapping them in white paper or shining tinfoil. As we go over to order a cheese and onion pizza – *fromage et oignon, seize francs* – sixteen francs, I feel the swelling heat of the oven overflowing over the counter out of the little van. I wonder how she stands it. Such work would be all right in the cold days of winter, but even in May, on a warm day, it must be sweltering in there. Satia asks her if she is there every Sunday. *Oui, madame, chaque dimanche, mai juin juillet et août* – every Sunday, all summer. The sweat runs down her bare arms, and when she bends down so that we can see her face she smiles showing her irregular teeth. Her body and arms and face are like a child's, she seems to me like a child, but the man who stands around outside the van, or lounges in the front seat reading a magazine, calls her *ma femme* – 'my wife'. It is as if the daily blasting heat of the oven in the tiny space of the little van had melted every bit of extra flesh from the body, had thinned her down to a minimum, to a proportion suitable for the available space and air and light. There she is now sliding a fresh pizza into the oven, now she slides another one steaming out again, now she is rolling out a chunk of dough under her wooden rolling-pin. But I am not sorry to have her work so hard in such cramped uncomfortable quarters : the smell of the pizza is wonderful, the taste is superb.

The long face of the Catalan women, long, slender, delicate and yet strong, the long oval of the face accented by the long drape of dark hair, falling straight back from the forehead, behind the ears, down along the shoulders and down the back, and from ear to slightly pointed chin the long graceful descending curve of the jaw, from ear to chin, and above the chin and mouth the long, slender nose. But not all is delicate, the face is saved from delicacy by the full lips, the large dark eyes, broad and full, filling the face. The old native dress is gone, they wear jeans, overalls, slacks, anything, like all the world, indistinguishable, but the face remains their own.

Light and shade alternate in the market square. The thin white cloth of a woman's nightgown hanging from the edge of the large square umbrella catches the bright sun and turns it into whiteness. The crippled vendor sits beside it in his chair, in the shade, but the metal rims of the wheels catch the sun and flash it back, the spokes outlined against the patches of sun and shade on the sand behind him. Where the sun falls on the sand the spokes appear dark by contrast before it, but where there is shade behind them the spokes seem bright and full of light. He folds knitted blouses and jokes with the women who stop. His wife arranges stockings, underwear, blouses, her smooth face, the perfection of her skin emphasized by her small, dark features, the tight bun on the back of her round head at the end of her fine straight hair. As people walk they move in and out of the uneven patches of sun and shadow, the light and colour of the market changing always as they move about, and above them the dark and light greenness of the leaves, the tan-grey blotched branches and trunks of the plane trees, the scattered glimpses of sky, sun.

People shop at the food stands, they are busy, but ignore the others, the vendors of bolts of cloth and oil-cloth, of kitchen things — strainers, pots, jugs, pitchers, clothes-pins, a hundred items — and clothing and shoes. There is a recession going on in France, there is too much unemployment, the local women do not have the extra coin to spend. They save it for food. How do the other vendors live?

*

21 May, p.m. We go to the 'African preserve' near Sigean. It is only 21 May but the sun is getting hot, when it is out. At the 'preserve' the brown bears are sluggish and roll over to sleep in the shade of the concrete wall. The rhinoceroses are a surprise, for all the pictures we have seen of them, a mysterious bulk of head that I would have put more with the dinosaurs than in our century. No doubt it is just

unfamiliarity. As we look we begin to assimilate them to other animals we have known. The ears are like pig's ears, their thick legs are like elephant's legs. The hump is like a bull's. But what about the two enormous protrusions on the front of their face, one just below the eyes, the other just above the stub nose? Tufts of hair grow from their ears. They are covered over with dry mud, they have obviously been bathing in it over their backs, or rolling in it, if they didn't seem too big to roll. As they graze the tall grass they shake off flies with a flick of their ears.

While we watch them a black bear sees us and approaches, his fore and hind legs seeming at first as if they were two different men, walking independently. The front leg never moves forward until the hind leg has come up to it, and that gives the black bear a wavy, sauntering walk. When his front part is moving left his rear part is moving right, and so on.

Surprised again at how lightly the rhinoceroses run, like huge heavyweight wrestlers gingerly bouncing on the balls of their feet on the stretched canvas of the ring. We wonder if they are a breeding pair, or of the same sex. One of them squats to piss, spreading her, or his, legs just the way a ewe would do. Three black bears come over to bait one of the rhinoceroses. They get up on top of the mound where he is grazing and taunt him with their paws, the way a cat does a dog, and then draw back. He makes butting gestures and movements hinting at threatening intentions with the point of his outer – larger – tusk, but it seems clear he is not serious, only annoyed. Finally he turns and trots off with his light, bouncing gait, catching up to the other rhinoceros. The two go off somewhere together.

It is hard not to humanize the lions. Nothing comes to mind so quickly as a royal court full of bored oriental philosophers – not bored, but rather tranquil, at ease, relaxed. But the frequent yawns give the impression of boredom. They sit and look off into the distance, hardly seeming to look. Where are the females? Ten or twelve males, but no females, so they try to make love to each other. After a spell of lying about and yawning they begin to get restless, wander about, get playful. A group of them are starting to play right ahead of where we are parked. An attendant, in a small white van, breaks it up by driving towards them.

Although there are little signs everywhere pointing out how much

41

better this reserve is than an ordinary zoo – *quelquonque zoo* – where the animals die of loneliness and too much confinement, it still seems to me to have many of the elements of a zoo. They have gone a long way towards reproducing the natural habitat, and the animals have more scope than usual, but they are still essentially caged. They cannot hunt, cannot seek their own food, or do anything that is natural to them. There is a whole group of leopards looking distinctly uneasy. The sign says they will only breed in large areas : they must have plenty of space around them. Privacy. In less than thirty acres or so of his own ground the male becomes sterile. Here they are, in a nice little park of an acre or two, a whole group of them. It is far better than a cage, but it is still imprisonment. So also with the lions, twelve males without any female. No doubt if a female were introduced among them now the males would tear each other apart.

The dromedaries eat hay, but do they ever get out to run? The Corsican *mouflons* – they look like a beautiful small breed of sheep, the rams with handsome horns – have their own enclosure of an acre or so, but it is sad to see them tearing at the tiny patches of grass eaten almost into the soil. Are they ever let out on to fresh grazing, or is their diet all hay? The hay looks green and tender, good quality, but the *mouflons* crave fresh grass. What must make it worse for them is that not far away there are acres and acres of tall, ungrazed grass. I am sure they smell it, and it torments them not being able to get to it. Worst of all, in this way of imprisonment, is the elephant. The signs say he was born in India in 1973. That makes him six years old, and he is still not very big. He is all alone, as far as we can see, and he paces restlessly back and forth in circles and lets out an angry growl every few minutes. It sounds like anguish. His condition seems a cruel one.

The alligators are apparently content. There are big signs up admonishing people not to throw stones into their enclosure. The alligators eat the stones and die of intestinal occlusion. How painful that must be! The sign goes on to explain that their torpid behaviour is perfectly normal – that explains the stones : people trying to get some activity out of them. They are fed once a week, the sign says, and spend most of the rest of the week digesting, their very low metabolism being designed by nature for the conservation of energy. We try to see them breathe, and can barely detect any sign of motion.

From time to time, at long intervals, an eyelid moves. Satia is sure they are watching us. Once we have accepted the fact that they are really alive their immobility has something very beautiful about it, and strange.

*

The phone remains an enigma. It all has to do with this mail strike in Ireland, which is now three months and one week old. I want to extend my Automobile Association Vehicle Recovery Policy. It only costs £2.00 a month, but there is no way I can contact the branch in Dublin where I took it out. Instead I decide to call the Automobile Association representative in Boulogne.

I am catching on to the direct-dial system well enough to get through to him without trouble. I explain what I want : I want to know whether I can send the money to him and have him renew my policy. Instead of answering that question he asks me whether I am calling from a pay-phone – he must be able to hear me putting the francs into the slot. I say I am.

'Where?'

'Near Perpignan' – a deliberate simplification, since I am really in Argeles.

'Go to the post office in Perpignan and ask the clerk for *libre appel*,' he says. 'Do you understand that? *Libre appel*, twenty-one-zero-one. It is a free service – *gratuit* – it won't cost you anything to make the call.'

I put in another franc and repeat that back to him just to make sure I got it right.

'That's right,' he says just before I hang up. '*Libre appel* twenty-one-zero-one – *service gratuit*.'

I go to the Argeles post office and, as usual, there is a long line waiting. Everybody is very patient. Obviously the French are not given to public grumbling. The young woman behind the counter is more overworked than ever. Tourists are arriving every day now that the good weather has started and her eyes are beginning to take on a sunken look. They have dark shadows around them. She looks even thinner. Shabbily dressed young men with beards present ragged identity cards and ask for *poste restante* letters which never seem to be there (she hardly appears even to look). Local people present packages for weighing and registering and putting stamps on. Pensioners wait to collect their pension money. The young woman twists around to her right to dial a number at the little switchboard next to and slightly behind her, then, still holding the receiver, twists back to her left to dial a stamp-label from another machine, licks the label, pastes it on to an envelope, picks up a large rubber stamp, inks it, and stamps a bold-lettered word on to an envelope: LETTRE.

My turn comes. Her jaw drops when she hears what I want. Her mouth hangs open in silent eloquence. *What does this foreigner want now?* her expression seems to say. She has never heard of *libre appel*. She shakes her head.

'Ask that old gentleman behind the other counter there,' I suggest in the clearest French I can manage. She looks towards him and he, sensing that something is going on, looks up. He has never heard of it either. She disappears into a back room, and when she comes back again several minutes later she has still never heard of it.

Non.

No point in trying the impossible. Instead I ask for a phone-booth – *une cabine* – you have to get permission to use one before you go ahead – and dial Boulogne again. I don't put in any coins but the units are ticking up on the meter on the little switch-board behind the young woman. The clerk in Boulogne recognizes my voice at once. 'Did you get *libre appel*,' he asks with a note of gladness in his voice. 'No,' I say, 'but perhaps you could just give me the information I need.'

'Wait a minute,' – he is like a bull-dog, tenacious, I can hear it in his voice – 'why didn't you get *libre appel*? You should be talking free.'

'I couldn't get *libre appel*,' I explain. 'The young woman here has never heard of it.'

'Never heard of it? Where are you? Are you in the post office in Perpignan?'

'No,' I explain, 'I am in the post office in Argeles-sur-Mer.'

'Not in Perpignan?'

'No. Argeles-sur-Mer.'

'And she has never heard of *libre appel*?'

'No.'

'Listen, put her on the line. Let me talk to her.'

I have a sense of units ticking rapidly away while we are having this conversation. I look through the glass phone-booth door and through the glass partition that separate me from where the young woman is sitting some ten metres away desperately trying to attend to the urgent needs of a line a dozen long.

'Give the phone to the clerk,' the man in Boulogne insists, impatient at my silence.

I still fail to find words. 'Impossible,' I say at last, wanting to drop the whole subject and get back to my Vehicle Recovery Policy.

'Impossible? Just ask her to take the phone and talk to me for a minute. I will explain *libre appel* to her.'

I make a quick calculation of just how much it is likely to cost me while he is paving the way for my free call. I think it is going to be too absurd, my going out and interrupting all those patient people on line waiting to cash their pension cheques and mail their packages and collect long-awaited (if non-existent) letters – butting in ahead of them (because the units are ticking away) and suddenly telling the young woman that there is a gentleman in Boulogne – *un monsieur à Boulogne* – who wants to talk to her. Her mouth will hang even more open, her sunken eyes look even more desperate.

'*Quoi – Un monsieur à Boulogne* – who wants to talk to me?' And the look : 'What does this foreigner want now?'

'Look,' I say. 'I can't do that. Why don't you call me here, here at the post office in Argeles?'

'Where are you?'

'I am at the Argeles-sur-Mer post office, six-six-seven-nought-nought Argeles-sur-Mer,' I say, giving the full postal code so he will know exactly where I am. 'Why don't you call me here?'

'What is the number of the phone?'

'The number of the phone?'

'Yes. What is the number of the phone at the post office?'

I look at the phone. There is no number on it. 'I don't know,' I say. 'You could look it up in the phone book.'

He pauses, then resumes. 'Look,' he says, 'just let me talk to the clerk. I will explain it to her.'

'There's no point in that,' I say. 'She wouldn't understand you,' and, within my own thoughts, I think I am beginning to see the way out of the labyrinth.

'Wouldn't understand? Why not?'

I pause for emphasis. 'Because she is *ignorant*,' I say.

Now the pause is on the other end. A pause of shocked silence – I can feel it, sense it. An insult to French national dignity, an actionable insult to a French civil servant! I can almost hear him gasp.

'Ignorant?!'

'Listen,' I say, 'let's forget *libre appel*. Why not just tell me what I have to send you to renew the policy? It will be cheaper in the long run forgetting about *libre appel* and just giving me the information.'

'O.K.,' he says, and he tells me: a cheque for £2.00 made out to the Automobile Association, a xerox copy of the policy I already have, a letter of authorisation.

'Is that all?' I ask, astonished. The whole telling of it had taken less than twenty seconds after all – a franc's worth of conversation.

'That's all. I'll send you the new policy.'

'Oh . . . thanks. Thank you very much,' I say. 'Thank you,' I add, and hang up. It was as simple as that.

*

23 May. We cross the Spanish border and go to Gerona. The cathedral square, all broad areas of high wall built of a light, warm stone. The bright sun emphasizes the way everything is arranged into planes, harmonious, contrasting. The same stone inside the cathedral is cool and dark, the obscurity broken only by the intensely coloured light of the high windows. Small areas of coloured light, more intense by contrast with the darkness. It is like a delicate jewel on a massive scale. Outside, the irregular sides of the cathedral cloister are a play of light and shade, the bright sun that falls into the courtyard shining back through the rounded arches on the walls of the arcade, reflecting again on to the inner faces of the sculpted capitals. We admire the little carved figures that are at the level of our eyes, the sequence of scenes telling their story: God extracting a slender, curving rib from Adam, Eve rising from the rib, Adam biting into a pomegranate, Adam and Eve crouching awkwardly trying to hide from wrathful God. Further on, Jacob perfectly sculpted in twelve inches of stone, sleeps on the ground, a stone for his pillow, while next to his head two tiny men, tiny but perfectly proportioned in their activity, rise and descend a short stout ladder

that links the very top and bottom of the scene on the capital. Above the sleeping Jacob a waking Jacob struggles, strangely tranquil, with an equally tranquil angel, their faces beautiful in repose. Next to these two images of himself another Jacob consecrates the stone that was his pillow, and yet another removes the heavy round stone that covers Rachel's well – the thirsty sheep look on admiring – and finally two perfectly sculpted small figures, Jacob and Rachel, meet in a chaste kiss. We admire the little narrative for a long time, then go on to the cathedral museum, where we find a tapestry from the eleventh century, a great wall-hanging in primitive but vigorous lines, repeating some of what we have just seen : God creates the world, the earth and the sea, light, fish, animals, man, the whole in simple, forceful drawing and colour that we call primitive but which we admire perhaps the more for that. The sacred story is surrounded by an earthly one, the four winds with winged feet astride huge bladders that exhale forceful currents of air, the seasons, and finally the men themselves for whom it all was done, created, the men busy at the works – and pleasures – of the turning year, hunting, fishing, ploughing, sowing, reaping, threshing, gathering the grapes from the vine, active in summer, shivering by the fire in winter, making the most of this great world.

In the afternoon we sit on the stone bench that runs along the side-portal of the cathedral and watch a hundred school-children play. The sun falls across the broad square from the southwest, the children jump rope, boys and girls alike, play handball against the side of the cathedral, skate, wrestle, run, skip about, sit and talk. The area of the square is broken up into different levels that pattern it into warm light and deep shade, and we try to take in everything we see before us : steps, façade, portal, sun, shadow, voices, shouts, calling of names, laughter, the running, jumping, little groups always varying, always in movement. The ball flies through the air, smacks the stone wall, returns to the waiting boys, their arms extended, palms open, eyes attentive, the jumping-rope swings up and down and around, the children skip in and out. Suddenly all stops, they gather into little clustered groups, into lines, the sunlight on their backs, their arms. At a signal they run, each line in its turn, back into the school, the sound of their voices diminishing as they run through the school door until the square is silent again and empty.

We drive to Besalú to see the Romanesque church there, find it on a broad open sun-filled square like the cathedral square at Gerona, but instead of a paving of stones this square is all dust, the dry yellow dust of Spanish summer. Two fierce and graceful lions arch high up above the church portal. Inside, the priest is rehearsing the village children in choral singing, accompanying them on the deep notes of the organ which sounds out fully under the perfect round arches and long stone vault of the church. School satchels and exercise books have been left lying on the wooden benches, the children stand gathered around the priest at the very front of the church to the right of the altar. We sit and listen to the singing, the soft, obedient voices, trying unsuccessfully in the soft light to make out the figures carved on the capitals that crown the tall columns.

Outside we find an attractive café at the very opposite corner from the church, its tables and chairs sheltered under an awning of straw from the still warm sun. Satia goes off to look for two buns to go with our coffee and I sit down at one of the tables to wait for her. The dust has left its fine powder over everything, tables, chairs. After a long interval a woman comes out to take my order and I tell her, in such Spanish as I can manage, that I am waiting for my wife to come back.

'Wait then,' she says, with what sounds a little like annoyance.

I look across the dusty square, the yellow dust, the warm afternoon sun, the young trees that have been planted around the edge of the square, the church, and hear the soft sound of the children singing in chorus. The singing stops, and after a while the children burst from the church and begin to run and play in the square, before the church. Two girls run after a third and try to pull up her dress. They all giggle and scream. The two are persistent, throw down their satchels, take hold of the other girl's skirts, try to pull them up, but she runs over to a tree, shelters against it, slides down to the ground, giggling. A boy runs over quickly and takes them by surprise. One of them is so intent on trying to pull up her friend's dress she does not notice the boy. He is wearing a bright green shirt and dark pants and his hair is very black. Quickly he throws the skirts of her light blue summer dress up over her head, runs away smiling and laughing. Instantly she runs after him, outrage and indignation on her face, her hand extended to slap, but he is too quick, he leads her around the square, runs in rapid irregular lines back and forth until she gives up, indignant, unable to catch him.

Satia returns with the buns and goes in to order the two coffees. After a few minutes she comes back.

'She is talking on the phone, and shows no sign of finishing,' she says.

She sits down and we wait. Finally I get up and go in. The woman is still on the phone. I decide to wait for her to finish. It is her café, after all, her country. She goes on talking. She talks, listens, talks. After a few more minutes she turns her head and looks at me and smiles slightly. I understand her look : 'Wait, then.' Reluctantly, we give up. The dusty yellow square is still full of sun, and there are no cars, no noise, only people, women with babies, children, old men limping slowly along leaning on their sticks.

*

Attrape-nigaud – 'sucker trap'. Madame Fissier has taught me the term apropos of the porcelain vendor who was selling Limoges china from a huge trailer-truck in the parking lot this morning. He started by giving away porcelain ash-trays to everyone, then serving-dishes to a lucky few, then a whole service to one woman, then by asking for a single franc in return, then for ten francs, then for thirty, then for fifty, then for a hundred. In the end he was offering dishes, crystal, table-cloth, napkins, silver-service, all for an 'astonishingly low price' which worked out to something in the region of a thousand dollars. I saw one man sign up.

*

I am still having trouble with the phone, trying to get through to Ireland. I wish the mail strike would end. I finally found a phone at Argeles-Plage – the beach – that works. At first I thought it was out of order, because it reacted differently from the others. All the other phones I have used start with a dial-tone, then when you dial nine-one, the *indicatif* for foreign calls, you get a series of chirping noises, or bleeps, which stop after a while. Then you go ahead and dial your number. This phone at the beach knows nothing of chirping-bleeping noises: instead it goes directly into a heavy, ominous drone.

'Broken!' I said to myself when I first used it. But then I went all the way in to Perpignan to try the post-office phones there – heavy with misgivings – and the woman there told me that that was the way it was supposed to be – a heavy drone – *une sonorité*.

The next time I went back to the phone at the beach there was a Frenchman using it – or, possibly, *not* using it, since he seemed to be getting nowhere when he dialled. The coins kept coming back with a loud rattle and he would groan and mutter and try again, until finally he gave up, pulled out his handkerchief and wiped off the sweat from his hands and face. '*Ça ne marche pas*,' he growled.

Je sais – 'I know,' I said. 'It's always like that.' However bad my accent those few words were sufficient inducement to him to explain to me, in voluble French, all the many difficulties he had been having with the phone. Impossible to get through. I'm not sure I understood everything he said, but I nodded my head in sympathy, getting the gist, thinking I understood at any rate, or perhaps just thinking of my own experiences while he talked. Then I tried the phone, shrugging mental shoulders. Astonishingly, it worked. I got through instantly, to Ireland.

From then on it was my phone, and whenever I really wanted to get through I went to it. Until one day I found a tall, muscular German tourist in shorts and tennis shoes – summer is here, I thought – telling someone at the other end – I just managed to follow the conversation – that he was near the Spanish border, one thousand four hundred kilometres from home, and that he had tried phone after phone and none of them worked, until he found this one.

Ha! I thought, that proves it. Waiting impatiently I listened attentively to the rest of the conversation, until at last I heard the approaches to the closing salutations, reluctant on his part, the final conclusive *Tucchüss, Tschüss*, the hanging up, the tinkling gathering of the unused coins into hand and pocket. He turned to go. The phone – *the* phone – was mine.

As before I got through at once. Anticipating the need to talk for more than a few seconds I fed in a five-franc piece instead of the usual one-franc ones. And just as I did, right in the middle of what my friend was saying, the phone went dead. Utterly dead – that dead sound of silence a phone has when it has decided to cut you off. Not only did it go dead, but it refused to work again under any circumstance. I hung up, tried again, put in coins, etc., etc., and could not get even the dial tone. Dead. Dead.

And that is when the illumination came, the insight. I drove back to Argeles to the parking lot, to the phones that *never* worked, put a coin into one of them, dialled my one-nine, listened to the series of chirping bleeps, let them go silent and then . . . waited. Yes, waited. And waited. Listening to the silence, listening, almost, for what it had to say. Until, astonishingly, I heard it, the other sound, the ominous buzz. The ominous buzz that is the go-ahead. So, there was nothing wrong with the phones after all. It was me who was to blame, using them incorrectly. Ah well, that's all right, I know I'm out of step with machines, with the machine world, but what about those other two, the Frenchman and the German? What about them? Are they both out of step too? Maybe most of us are out of step.

*

Theme: The innumerable languages of sound that we ignore as communications. Bird song, inarticulate human sound, animal noises – but also phone bleeps and tonalities (which are like colour codes in sound), and – in a strange way – the buzz and hum of traffic, the neighbour's TV, etc. A communication theme.

*

22 May. The *Monde* carries an article on the back page: DISSATIS-FACTION IN ALSACE OVER THE EUROPE-PRIZE FOR BARRE AND SCHMIDT.

It seems that Barre and Schmidt, the Prime Ministers of France and Germany, are to receive four hundred thousand francs for 'meritorious contribution towards building a unified Europe.' The *Monde* says there is 'a certain difference of opinion' about this prize. 'There is even a certain annoyance in Alsace, and a feeling that all is not right,' the article adds. The prize itself was set up by a rich grain-merchant of Hamburg. What particularly disturbs the Alsacians, the French-speaking ones, anyway, and especially 'those injured in the war, veterans, members of the resistance movement,' is that the German grain-merchant is also a generous supporter of the autonomist movement in Alsace, with a strong emphasis on the Teutonic qualities of the region.

I cannot quite make out from the article whether they also object to their Prime Minister collecting a fat cheque – something like a hundred thousand dollars – for carrying out national policy – doing his job, in short. In any event, I understand the annoyance, and the growing cynicism that I hear people here complain of.

*

Invited to 'coffee' by Monsieur and Madame Fissier, it turns out to be more like a little celebration with their friends the Barbes. Monsieur Barbe is an *ancien pilote* – he forms his hand into wings, makes a buzzing noise with his mouth, and flies his hands about in acrobatics – who gave up flying at his wife's request and became a civil servant, then a liquor salesman. The conversation begins with jokes, witticisms, laughter, then gradually turns to how good the apricot pie is, how good the coffee is, the sparkling white wine, and so on; how little everyone cares for tea (which comes up because we have been living in Ireland); then a long discussion of the cherries which Madame Fissier has picked at the near-by campsite and brought in in a large bowl; then on to popular entertainers, singers, cabaret; then on to movies; then on to pornographic movies; then on to the children and 'how well they are doing'; then to 'how bad times are' – that theme that never fails, even in the best of times; then ('no politics') on to politics, criticism of American 'domination' of Europe (so that we have to remind them of their *liberté*); then on to illnesses, faith-healing, personal-magnetism cures, hypnotism, fear of death, the afterlife, the resurrection, eternity, etc., breaking down finally into genuine small talk, the radishes, the trout in the cistern, the cherries, the cucumbers, and so on until the goodbyes.

*

This fishing-net, the net of one of the fishing boats at St Cyprien, lying folded and refolded in long lengths upon itself, it could be covering a sleeping giant – there the hips, there the shoulder, the head, the arms, there the legs, all in repose. How many textures of net are there? One, two, three, four . . . the finest parts of the net, the narrow mesh, like layers of veils folding over and upon themselves over and over, transparent and yet, by reason of the many folds, opaque, thin and fine, yet making this thickness and bulk, a heap ten feet long, five wide, three high. The sea has aged the net, taken the brightness from its colours, given it all a patina of greyness, dullness, so that what was once a bright wine colour is now a dull earth red, more brown than red, but never the same as itself for long, inch by inch changing, modifying, darker, lighter, browner, paler, more pink, more grey, until it has lost its red and brown and all the colour that remains is a pale pink, a pale earth pink, a shade of faded copper where the weak sun catches its folds, and then even that colour is gone, and the mesh is grey, grey and dull white. But further on it reappears in twists of ochre, soft ochre and faded tones of rust swirling together in static movement. Over the fine mesh lies the heavier more open net, and finally the heaviest of all, a heavy orange mesh, and the chain, splotches of white and brown rust on grey metal. The ropes twist back and around. The round cork floats of the net are like its fruit, a fruit of huge berries, or else like giant strings of coral beads.

*

A flat fish, he lies flat on the table, his body spread out like a flat-iron, long and tapering, broad and almost round in front, and then narrowing towards the tail, but always flat. It is as if in front he were all face, all round flat face, and from the back of the face comes the little body, the torso, dwindling rapidly into a narrow, fine tail. In a way he is like a kind of dwarf, his head the most of himself. And all this flat, only slightly rounded upper surface is brown, a dull brown that masks and covers the pearl-pink undertones of his flesh. At the very front, beyond a fringe of boldly curving chin, curving like the prow of a powerful tug, the broad mouth, open, almost as though in a grin, the upper jaw pulled back like a grinning lip, the pearl pink-grey mouth open to the oncoming current, and the whole mouth fringed with little sharp teeth, sharp little brown and pink

53

teeth pointing backwards, inwards, not to chew but to catch, to stop the escape from that gaping chamber. The delicate black and grey lines, threads, that should float upwards in the water lie flatly pasted now against his body, flat and dead on the table. His dead eyes, mounted one each just to the side of the double spine that runs back from the middle of the lifted upper jaw, look up and slightly outwards. He caught his prey from below, he coasted the bottom of the sea looking upward, perceiving perhaps no more than a shape, a form, and then instantly darted upward like a living wing, gliding swiftly upward through the water, seizing the prey with the gripping teeth that could not release if they would. Those two fins, flat like black flippers, coming out backwards and only slightly sideward from what must be his shoulders – the flat areas that look like muscle, at the sides right where the flattened head meets the strong, solid little body – those two flat flipper-like fins were what propelled him suddenly forward, upward, for the catch. The fin on the back of the little torso held him balanced on an even plane, and the vertical tail-fin like a rudder steered him right and left, and when he moved through the water he was like a wing. But I think those three long black threads that rose from his nose and upper jaw were what really perceived the prey, felt the prey, and that the large, gaping yellow and dark blue eyes only sensed a shadowy form above him, a general place to aim.

*

The wind is blowing through the leaves of the trees, a soft, continuous sound, the grass is tall and waves in the wind, a pattern of green light and shade in the bright sun. There are many cattle in the field, fifty at least, possibly more, all still, almost all of them resting, lying down, chewing their cud, they lie in the sun and shade of the plane trees, or in the open sun, sideways on to wind and sun, both of which are coming from the same direction. The town in the distance is brown stone and mud, the tan walls harmonize with the red tiles of the roofs. The square church tower stands above all the houses of the town, but one building is higher than the rest, it is like a rustic castle. If there is any noise from the town it is lost in the wind as I watch the peaceful cows resting in the tall grass.

54

The slope of the brown cow's back when she rests, lying with her four legs folded under her, the front legs folded back, the rear legs folded forward. Her spine is slightly to one side. It does not run directly down the centre of her resting body but always slightly to one side. Her weight is gently shifted. Lying on the grass she is mostly body, a huge, capacious body and only a little head, and the slope of her back that I see is really the gentle swelling rise of her left flank, the curve of a ribbed flank rising above her spine. Her back is a long curve, with gentle undulations, that goes from the strong low hump of her shoulder to the final rounding curve of her tail, itself folded around and in to her body, like her legs. I cannot see her hind legs at all, but her folded forelegs support the forward part of her weight, and from them loose folds of skin lead up in waves to her head and chin, her slowly moving jaw rising and falling with a turning, circular motion as it slowly, rhythmically chews the cud. She stops, the chewed cud descends in a lump that I can follow with my eyes moving down her throat. She waits. Another lump rises up. She starts to chew again with the same slightly circular, turning movement of the jaw. Her ears, back towards her neck, are full of a long fur of hairs, her short horns curve out only six or eight inches, her eyes are dark, black, with black bristles around them for lids. She unfolds one foreleg, then folds it in again, all the while peacefully chewing her cud.

*

We drive to Casteil for the walk up to Saint-Martin-du-Canigou. The open café, its smoking grill, smoking still with the remnants of the lunch-time fire, the red umbrellas over the tables, a man in a grey cotton shirt with a bulging belly takes the orders, four people sit at a table near us, order lemonades, change their minds when they see the tiny bottles, order beer instead. They are farmers, we think, they are like the farmers we know in Ireland : the two men, their tall faces, long noses, large ears, big hands, overhanging brows, small bright well-protected eyes; the two women : tall, broad, broad shoulders, full bellies, powerful arms, big buttocks, the younger one her hair frizzled and curled, her broad face, the work she has done — how many children ? They talk and laugh, smiling broadly, looking around and smiling at us as they laugh, as though the good joke belonged to everyone, belonged to us too. One of the men takes a camera from the pocket of his leather jacket. The other, dark-blue suited, with a dark blue pullover up to the collar of his white shirt, takes the camera. The three who are to be photographed sit all on one side of the table, the man with the camera goes several yards off, folds his long body, sits on some steps, holds the camera to his tilted head, squints, grins showing his large, strong teeth, twists up his face. Much laughter, joking. The older woman puts on powder and lipstick. More squinting, grinning. Finally the shutter clicks – Done! – the camera back in the pocket, all sit easily around the table again, try the beer, the jokes subside, they fall silent. At last the jeep they have been waiting for comes. That is what they have been waiting for, the jeep to take them to Saint-Martin-du-Canigou.

They are taking the jeep, but we prefer to ascend the steep, narrow mile and a half on foot, the traditional way. That is half the interest in the monastery, we think, and we regret the availability of jeeps. A minute later a little French car goes by too. We look our surprise to the man in the grey cotton shirt. Is it becoming a general thing to take cars up the path to the monastery? He shakes his head quietly.

'He is going to come back,' he says. *Il va reculer.* 'You'll see, in a minute.' He is right. We don't wait long before we see the little car going the other way.

We set off ourselves on foot along the narrow path. In a minute or two we hear a roar of sound around the bend ahead of us. It is like the roar of traffic. Is it the jeep returning? We turn the bend and see the foam of a white cataract hundreds of yards – already – below us. Across from us the yellow-grey rock rises in steep out-croppings like monster chips of stone escalading vertically to the high peaks, with trees, their foliage fresh green, growing from every little shelf or ledge.

We walk on upward along the steep path. Further on we look into a high mountain valley, the tiny dots of colour in a distant sloping pasture are the grazing cattle. Further up, at last we just see the top of the square stone tower through the trees, crenellations, weathered yellow stone, the four round-arched windows near the top in double pairs. My armpits ache from the climb, the strain on my lungs. A cool wind blows through the leaves, a bird's call has a short, metallic note, the intervals between the little double notes are always the same. He is whistling through his throat.

The end of the church shoulders the side of the square tower, bulging its four apses towards the east, not symmetrically but a larger apse in the middle and a smaller one to each side. The fourth is added on beside the other three, an afterthought. A high narrow window in every apse.

Everywhere there are signs appealing for quiet. Learn to hear the message of silence with us. Do not disturb our peace. We hear the sound of the jeep, soon we see it rounding the angle above us, then a second, then a third, this time with the people from the café. I wave and the man with the camera waves back, sharing his good time with the world.

Behind the monastery the mountain rises up, steeply up, upward. The predominant idea is verticality, verticality dominates the backdrop to the monastery, not just the grey stone rising in massive chips of fissured rock, stained here and there in flowing descending lines of yellow rust; the trees that have planted themselves on to the narrow shelves, their foliage many greens now at the end of May, lighter and darker, yellow greens and orange greens; and where the trees have not been able to take hold, where the ledge is too small, the bright yellow broom, round clusters of the yellow flowers; or where the broom cannot take hold the coarse grass, lines of grass pushing out along the fissures of the rock. Is it the grass that breaks the stone, causes the rock to fall, opening larger fissures and shelves for the broom, the broom for the trees? Giant chips of weathered grey stone lie about in steep layers, strangely stopped in their downward slide. We look upward and upward. Bushes and trees, stunted by wind and weather, grow even from the highest peaks of grey rock. And beyond those rocks, a further peak, the highest, furthest bit of mountain we can see, dark evergreens along its steeply mounting face and snow lying about yet along the crevices, between the trees. It is as if this were the steep road to heaven, this monastery perched here somewhere between earth and heaven, a half-way stage, the mountain and the rocks a visual reminder of the steepness of the way, the climb. If we are half-way there when we are here, how much there is yet to go, how steep! Across from where we stand, its sound a constant backdrop to our thoughts, a narrow cataract of white water falls in long descending steps.

Within the monastery all is pure curving arch, the pure half-circle arch of the Romanesque, the arcade of the cloister, the roof though wood its massive beams supported by three perfect arches of the light tan stone, the side walls themselves a structure of round arches, seven on the inside, nine on the side towards the mountain. The heaviness of stone made light, allowing light to pass through into the enclosed space. On the outer side, the side that faces towards the mountain and the white cataract, the nine arches are lighter still, resting not on pillars of cut stone but on slender columns, each with its carved base below and sculpted capital above. The columns are round, but some have been shaped into flat-faceted octagons, their capitals a strange theatre of enigmatic characters and events. Here what seems at first to be a series of two-headed lions, a head coming out of each end of their square bodies, a head at the front and a head at the back, but when I look closer I see that they are four separate lions, one for each face of the capital, cheek to rump, cheek to rump, cheek to rump all the way around, their manes lying in perfect braids behind their tiny ears and along their stout necks. Their thick legs and finely sculptured paws barely appear to touch the ground, so lightly are they suspended that they seem to dance, a delicate circular dance around the capital. Some grin broadly, a menacing and yet a harmless grin of fierce teeth, one hangs its long tongue, its length emphasized by a central crease, out from his open mouth. And above and behind each lion's body, right above the torso, the ribs, a long-chinned female face, the lips pursed and contained, the smooth high cheek-bones and long, rounded tapering chin deliberately taciturn, containing its secret. The faces are framed within two swirling scrolls, one to either side, and where the two scrolls meet, at the angles of the faces of the capital, a shell-like button perched squarely on each lion's head. And to balance each head, just below it, pasted against the very middle of the lion's broad body, something very like the end of a palm-frond – it is the tip of the lion's tail, curving around unseen from behind, under his body and up again to end at last right in the centre of this marble composition.

At the next column the half-naked bodies of three dancing-girls emerge from the faces of the capital, dancing with curving sabres above their heads, a sabre in each hand, the tips of the curving, well-formed blades meeting above their heads, their tiny arms diminished to accommodate them to the limited space of the capital, their faces hard, impassive, the lips tight, the small breasts high, and then a broad expanse of swelling belly above the casually twisted robe of cloth that covers and hides their short legs, only the points of their tiny feet appearing upon the very base of the capital. A bearded musician at the angle holds his slender viol but does not seem to play, looking off into the distance, a twisting dog-like monster at his feet. Another dancing-girl, her proportions, like the first, distorted to accommodate her to the space (her long belly, her dwarf legs and arms) dances on another dog. A third, facing outward to the mountains, is fully dressed, holds a block of wood or stone – or is it a box? – over her head, frowns severely, her mouth the section of an inverted bowl.

On another capital the lion theme is varied by eight large hawks, their wings folded, their bodies bent and curved slightly forward, two to a face, their wings a flowing design of parallel furrows and ridges, between them thick-faced bearded men, the scrolls that rise from their shoulders like angels' wings.

Another. The menacing flattened neck and tiny heads of cobras reduced to an almost perfect design in the red and white stone. This time the faces between are set on fluted columns, and above the ends of the wings grinning animal faces, Egyptian dogs.

And still another with odd animal-like men sitting back on unseen stools absorbed within the stone, leaning their hands on their animal knees, their faces gaping like hungry fish. Between them, standing on their fore-paws, rear legs descending to their shoulders, long flat tongues hanging out and down, four acrobatic dogs.

And so on through an assortment of strange animal shapes and winged faces to a capital of monks, a procession of monks, long-robed, their faces tranquil, slightly smiling, the little, contained mouths of the cloistered, one swings a censer suspended on three swirling chains, one carries a tall wooden cross, holding it carefully erect, like his own body, like the erect, careful robed stature of all the monks in the procession, the next holds a candle, and then three together side by side hold the fringed, tasselled altar-cloth, its surface neatly embroidered with the dove of peace, the olive branch flowing upward and backward from its beak.

A design of shells surmounted by two twisting serpents, each biting the other's tail. Finally, four long-legged lions, but with only two heads this time, two for all of them, each head shared by two bodies, two bodies to each jolly grinning head. The legs are long, the paws touch the ground lightly, very lightly, and the hind legs are so much longer than the forelegs that the lions seem to be bowing gracefully in their dance, their tails swirl under their bellies and out along their flanks, and between the forelegs of two of them, under the shared grinning head with the large teeth, a flatly sculpted smiling human face.

I follow the arcades of the irregular cloister around to where the narrow stone steps run up to the little church. Inside I count the twelve arches, six to a side, that separate the side aisles from the central nave, and all is arc, arches and vaults in perfect arcs supporting the heavy stone, the semi-circular apses that end the nave and aisles, the tall narrow arched windows. The six arches on either side are in pairs of three, the pairs separated by heavy pilasters of massed stone. The other arches rest on grey columns, not straight but bulging outward as they rise, then tapering again after the bulge, topped by grey capitals that spread outward and upward receiving the heavy weight of stone vault and arch on their broad upper surface, tapering it then to concentrate it all on the round column.

A monk in layman's clothing appears. He is the abbot of the small monastery and he offers a guided tour of the buildings. He talks about the history of Saint-Martin-du-Canigou, its founding around the year 1000, its abandonment eight hundred years later, its rediscovery half in ruins early in this century, the work of rebuilding. As he talks he sees that I am watching him more than the stones he is talking about, thinking that his liveliness belies his age. His skin is smooth, almost without a wrinkle, like that of a young man, but the spareness of flesh already reveals the skull beneath, suggests the coming of the end of life. It is a strange combination in a man so lively. It is as if a worldly abstinence had resulted in a physical youngness but a spiritual ageing, a spiritual ripeness. It seems to me that I am seeing a monk for the first time ever, a true monk.

Reading something of my thought as he catches my eye, the abbot talks briefly about himself. He is seventy-five and for thirty years he has lived, most of the time alone, in the remote monastery. A large part of the reconstruction has been done by his own hands, with the occasional help of young volunteers. There are photographs of himself and them at work.

In spite of his age I notice that he still climbs steps with the agility of a young man, leaps swiftly on to a balustrade to explain the carving on a capital, a detail of the architecture. I would like to engage him in conversation but the spareness and economy of his face and physique extends to his talk as well. Having finished a concise tour of the monastery he quickly disappears.

*

VILLE DE COLLIOURE
La Municipalité communique
à partir du Vendredi 1er Juin
la signalisation
(stationnement et circulation)
devra être respectée

CITY OF COLLIOURE
By order of the Mayor :
from Friday, June 1st,
traffic and parking
regulations
must be obeyed.

*

Sunday, 27 May. The market in Collioure. No sun, cloudy sky, dull. How dull it seems, this southern market place without its sun. And then the sun comes out and even in the weak sun the market is full of life again. The south of France lives from the sun, it has been made for the sun, with the sun in mind. The houses, the open spaces, the trees, the towns and streets, the people, their clothes, all have the sun in mind, and when there is no sun everything disappears, becomes flat, dull. Then the sun comes out and you see movement, people moving about, moving through patches of light and shade, a young woman walks past a market stand, the shade of a leaf of the plane tree moves across her brown, wavy hair. A man carries wooden fruit boxes through the thick pattern of light and shade.

The pattern itself is never still as the breeze moves the leaves back and forth, the light shimmers through the changing space, shining on the dusty ground. Beyond the tall thick plane trees a light ochre house, a pink house, a white house. An English woman and her son park their rented bicycles beside a tree and go off to see this market. The sound of Arabic calls my attention to a group of dark-skinned men coming in, smiling, laughing. A German voice, and then the mixed sounds of Catalan and French. The smells of olives and of pizza. The lazy coming and going of Sunday shoppers, lookers. Earlier on it is livelier, when people are shopping in earnest, buying, but now it is mostly just looking, strolling, passing the time.

*

A young man killed in the electric chair in Florida, says the *Aurore*. At 4.07 p.m. the Supreme Court in Washington confirmed the sentence of death, at 4.11 p.m. they strapped him in the chair, at 4.18 the official announcement of his death. Here in Collioure the sun is shining, people are swimming, we sit and drink coffee and watch the swimmers, the boats, the church, the sea. Is he at rest? I can't help feeling he has lost something.

*

Madame Fissier talks about the last night of the German occupation. Monsieur Fissier had dug a kind of trench for his wife and for his mother and father. She was twenty years old at the time and was nursing her first child, a daughter, only eight days old. They spent the night in the trench for fear of the nastiness of the last retreating German troops, but when daybreak came they were still afraid to go out. Finally they heard the church-bells ringing. It was the sign of the liberation. The Germans had left, the Americans had come. 'I went to sleep under German occupation, I woke up liberated,' she comments.

*

Post office, Argeles, to mail a postcard, strange kind I got in Dublin, entirely blank, no print, just a white card with rounded corners. I am twelfth in line. Everybody waits patiently. The young woman is working harder than ever, and faster. What good humour she is in! She examines the address on packets to be sent, consults long lists of postal rates, makes complicated calculations on her pocket computer, announces the price, puts the end of her ball-point into her mouth, adjusts the knobs on the postage machine, pulls a lever, tears out the freshly printed plain-paper stamp, takes her ball-point out of her mouth, licks the back of the newly printed stamp, pastes it on the packet, hammers it with the side of her fist, collects the money, looks up at the next person, and so on. No wonder the *Monde* has an article on too few post office clerks and too much work. When my turn comes I show her the postcard, indicating the address, waiting for the stamp. She looks at the postcard blankly, fails to recognize it as a postcard, looks at me. '*Vous voulez téléphoner?*' she asks sadly. 'No,' I say, 'it's a postcard.' Surprise and relief. '*Alors c'est un franc.*' She gives me the one-franc stamp and turns to the next in line.

*

I have a swim at Argeles and then drive up to Saint-Cyprien in search of the *naturistes* Madame Fissier has told us about, carefully following her directions – turn right at such and such a billboard, follow the road around past the campsite, and so on, and finally I arrive at some deserted dunes. Parking next to a lone Citroën I mount a dune and look right and left. The beach is almost deserted but in the distance in both directions I see small groups of properly costumed bathers. The only nude figures I see are a very small girl and an alsatian dog. Then I notice a young woman sun-bathing at the foot of the dune I am standing on, her round breasts exposed to the sky. I go to a deserted spot on the beach and grill in the warm sun. The salt from the swim hardens on to my skin. I can feel it intensifying the heat of the sun.

*

Madame Fissier brings us something different every day, asparagus, cherries, radishes, apple tarts, sorrel soup, and so on and on. Although the rent at all the campsites and commercially let apartments goes up in June, ours stays the same. That is in honour of our being the first tenants ever in the new apartment. And Monsieur Fissier says simply they are glad to have us as tenants. *Vous êtes les premiers* – 'You are the first ones.'

*

The work-horse drinks and his ears flick in rhythm to his drinking. With each swallow his ears move, as though he were twitching away flies. He snorts for more water and his owner brings another large bucket, leans it on the iron bar of the stall, at the level of the horse's mouth. The horse drinks, takes a small mouthful of hay, dribbles water from his mouth, working his jaws, tongue, cleaning his mouth. A small bowl of clean oats in the feed-box. The horse eats thoughtfully, intent.

The heavy beams of the stable ceiling. The ladder. A cat appears from the loft opening, hesitates on the uppermost rung, looks, descends, cautious. A dog with bells ringing runs past the cat, drinks from the bucket. Hay and straw lie about, dung. Vine-prunings in neat bundles. Chased by the dog the cat re-ascends the ladder. The two men talk in Catalan, leaning on the cart. The natural light and dark of the stable – rare now.

*

Perpignan. Place Arago. Sitting on one of those strange benches made of a single piece of iron, curved around to make a seat and a back, with round holes the size of coins stamped out all over them, so that only the framework is left. Is there a use for all those iron discs? Or is it just cheaper to do it that way? Are all the round pieces melted down again and re-used? A woman is resting against the back of the bench where I am sitting – so I have to sit leaning forward as I write – waiting for her bus to come along. But she was there first in any event.

The large bronze statue, now dark green, of Francis Arago standing in the attitude of an orator in frock coat and with his right arm extended in an authoritative gesture, dominates the square, or would dominate it if anyone noticed it. I have the feeling that no one does and I only notice it because I see the pigeons roosting on the little bronze reliefs of scenes from Arago's life, roosting on the arm of the little bronze Arago in his youth – *Premières études*, the inscription says – roosting on the head of the aged Arago as he leans against his desk – *Derniers travaux* – the bottoms of the reliefs white with pigeon droppings. At the bottom of the monument a coal-black pigeon squats on the marble base. A sports-car blasts its piercing trumpet horn behind my head, impatient to tear off through the traffic of cars, buses, cycles. The bus comes and the woman leaning on the back of the bench gets on it. I lean back.

A bus stops with screeching brakes. Old men stand around leaning against the enclosure that runs around the monument or sitting on the black iron bars, talking loudly, gesturing, their arms raised, fingers lightly extended in a gesture of affirmation, authority, much like that of the statue. One moment they are joking, laughing, another moment and they are serious, angry. They raise their arms part way, as high as their shoulders, and swing their clenched fists downwards as though pounding an imaginary table. But the anger remains for only a moment. Expressed, it subsides. Someone else takes the stage.

Old people sit on the benches around the square. A young man walks by in front of me, a young woman carrying her shopping bags comes along, puts them down by the bus-stop. People gradually accumulate to wait for the bus. In between the benches thick-trunked palm trees are growing, in front of them orange trees, without fruit now.

*

Monsieur and Madame Fissier come to the door just as we are about to leave for Perpignan, ask us if we want to go and pick cherries at the campsite with them. I had forgotten that we agreed to go with them – in fact, I had actually suggested it to Madame Fissier, because she found it too much work picking cherries by herself. Yet she has been doing so for days, always giving a lot to us. Satia says we are going to Perpignan, then we remember the appointment and go after them. We get to the tree and find there are still a lot of ripe cherries, but they are out of reach. I go back to get the ladder and I get the metal step-ladder because it is lighter than the wooden double one.

The ladder not the right one – back for the wooden one – Monsieur Fissier puts it against the tree and picks cherries – the old woman from the *mas* comes along and chats – the old man, her brother – they water their garden – talk about weeds: *arracher les mauvaises herbes* – drinking tea with the Fissiers – his recollection of his last cup of tea (also, in fact, his first) almost thirty-nine years ago to the day – 1 June, 1940, in England, after not having eaten for three days. Six days in England – English hospitality – the first thing was the cup of tea with milk, sugar and biscuits – offered a bath and clean underwear – taken to a night club full of people all singing and drinking champagne. His feelings: France overrun with Germans, in France there is war, here it is as if there is no war. The next day he returned to France.

We discuss the situation in Spain – internationally encouraged terrorism.

*

Place de Verdun. The café, the plane trees. A weak sun. The morning was misty, the sun only came out in the late afternoon. The tables near the centre of the café are all taken so I go further along, near the great brick monument, slightly removed from the centre of the stage which is the Place de Verdun. The inside of the café is closed off by large glass doors – they are almost entirely glass, they could be called glass walls – and as I look through them I see the reflection of the outdoor scene behind me even more vividly than I do the people seated inside the café. It is another stage. The glass is a flat surface but the people reflected in it seem just as far away from me as they would if I were looking directly towards them. The reflection in the glass is a perfect representation of everything before it. In some ways it is more so, because it has been reduced to a composition, it fixes the attention, people arrive, appearing in the distance, grow larger as they walk towards the foreground, keep growing larger until they dominate the scene and then pass quickly out of it while others take their place. The dark interior of the café adds another harmony, darkening the light, reducing the contrasts. But the scene reflected in the window is interrupted by the one that comes through the window from inside, the people sitting, static, at the inside tables, talking, reading newspapers, thinking, staring blankly ahead of themselves.

Now I see that I am also looking right through the café and out the other side to the brightly lighted window of a shoe-shop. Scores of women's shoes – black, tan, white – are displayed. The shoes appear through the bodies of a young man and woman who walk towards me out of the café window. My attention shifts from the transparent images of the walkers in the glass to the solid sitters within the café. It is as if the real people in the café were dreaming the scene in the glass. A man puts his hand to his chin in a gesture of doubt, uncertainty, reflection, just as a young woman carrying a small child passes across his face, over his shoulders, diminishing into the distance behind him as she walks. Her transparent image is walking towards the shoe-shop, her body dissected by its brilliantly lighted sign she walks into and beyond the sign, the shop, into an area of darkness – darkness of the café, the glass – where her reflection suddenly in a patch of sun becomes bright, opaque, becomes more real than the real people in the dark café, than the real backdrop of the shoe-shop. She walks for a moment in the sunlight and then disappears behind a passing car. It is as if the car is going to hit her, but instead it passes in front of her – of her image. The man in the café whose shoulders she walked across takes his hand from his chin, shifts his weight in his chair, looks around blankly. (It is like the stage of life, where people are always close to each other but unaware of one another; the scene a symbol of the troubled thoughts of the man in the café.)

*

30 May, Satia's birthday – must take the day off, but – how do you take the day off when you are on holiday anyway? There is no sun this morning and the clouds dampen enthusiasm. Then about 10.30

the sun appears and we drive to the beach. But in the final half mile the sun begins to look weak and by the time we have parked and are walking towards the sand it has gone away altogether. A dense mist is blowing in off the sea, densely white, enveloping. People are in rapid retreat and we notice that the mist is also chilly, penetrating. The visibility diminishes rapidly as the mist envelopes everything, the sea, the wooden poles that stick up out of the sand, the little shacks, even the trees along the promenade. The chopping sound of a helicopter, growing louder, coming nearer. It seems very near but we do not see it, stand waiting for it to appear. Louder. Finally we see it bright red but dim in the mist, skimming the beach, yards above the sand. What is he looking for?

When the sun returns we go back to the beach, lie on the sand near the water. The mist has gone but the wind is still strong, blowing in steadily off the sea.

It is hard to see the sea. Its troubled surface glistens in a million spots with warm yellow sunlight, and where it doesn't reflect back sunlight it reflects the pale blue sky or the flat white clouds. It is hard to see the sea itself, the salt water, and not the reflecting surface or the thing reflected. Mostly it is reflected light I see, transformed by the underlying colour of the water, but I do not see the sea itself. Only near the crests of the innumerable little waves is there a kind of darkness that might be the sea itself. I almost think that I can see through the dark crests of the waves into the water itself – a kind of transparency. But the flashing spots of sunlight blind me and I see only a kind of greyness-greenness, that and the repeated, self-renewing white roll of foam where the little waves curl on to the wet flat sand, bubbling, splashing rolls of white foam. And I hear the uninterrupted pattern of sound, the intervals never quite the same, always slightly different, so that there is no rhythm. My ear seeks a rhythm but the restless changing pattern of the surf defeats it, its soft growl a modest menace only of what it can be. It is like a wild animal dozing, held in check, but it reminds me of a night when I slept beside the sea, a winter night in Greece, on an island. I was inside a stone hut, sleeping on a bed of thyme, in a sleeping-bag, and the sea was thirty good feet down a cliff and another thirty away along the pebbly beach after that, and it only came in in a bay, a small bay you could swim across in two or three minutes, protected as well by natural jetty-like outcroppings of rough conglomerate rock, but in the middle of the night the wild roaring of wind and sea woke me up. I woke up in a kind of terror, a fright, for I had never heard a sound like it. I had heard storms before, even at sea, but there was something special about the sound of the sea that night. It was more than the fierce whistling of the wind and the fierce smashing of the waves against the rocks and the pebbly beach, the drawing up of the pebbles into the retreating waves and smashing them back again upon the shore with the sea's hoarse growl. It was that there was a purpose in the sound: the sea had a purpose, I could tell, it was demanding something. And although I knew it was mad I had a powerful desire to roll up my sleeping bag and flee, flee inland as fast as I could run. But I didn't, because I said to myself that it was mad, and I would be laughed at, so I stayed put, listening to the wild, covetous sound of the storm, thinking that it sounded as if it wanted to overreach itself, reach up to my little stone hut and take me back with it. In the morning the sea was calm, but when I went along the coast to the island port I found people in little groups, their talk perturbed, their faces troubled. In the middle of the night, just at about the time I had been awakened by the storm, the sea had swallowed up an island steamer. No one quite knew whether a truck in the hold had broken its moorings and smashed a hole in the side of the hull or whether the hull itself, too rotten from age to withstand the pounding, had simply opened up and swallowed the raging water, but they were certain that it had taken only a matter of minutes, a few minutes at the most, for the ship to go under. No one I talked to had heard the sound of the sea during the night. They had slept through it. Remembering my own sensations I imagined those of the people on the steamer — within limits: even in imagination the terror is too strong. Now, sitting on the beach here, I only hear the subdued mutter of the sea through the hiss of the wind against my ears and the laughing shouts of the English bathers.

*

Collioure port. The little boy on the winch. The winch is rusted, a smooth rust, the rust of old iron. For the little boy it is a ship —

69

bateau atomique – an atomic ship, and to him it seems just the right size to be a ship for a little boy, and sufficiently varied: the tapering vertical cylinder of the winch itself, the platform around it, the chain that secures the lid that covers the control-levers. The little boy, his hair blond, straight and long enough to reach the collar of his white shirt, his short trousers striped white and grey, white tennis shoes, runs around on the platform, squats behind the winch, gives orders to the crew, calls down observations from the look-out tower and simultaneously takes note of them, gives new orders, navigates, aims – FIRES – torpedoes, cannons, bombs, rockets, rifles, pistols, machine-guns – *atomique!* – and creates the appropriate noises, the explosions, the spouting water, the shattering metal of the wounded vessel, the sinking ship, the falling plane – the cannon fires and the bomb bursts, his mouth spits out the sounds, sharp, hollow, dull, loud, blasting in turn, a great variety of weapons and their effects, running around the winch, squatting, rising, describing the action as he goes, sighting the enemy, manoeuvring. An action reaches its peak and then suddenly he is silent, pauses, an intermission in the battle, until slowly the battle resumes with intermittent firing, sporadic rifle-shots, gradually intensifying, growing more frequent, louder, the cannons again, the torpedoes, bombs, explosions, the multiple noises, deep, high, loud, soft, liquid – the sea-battle, all with the many running commentaries on the action, the description that makes it real. At last he subsides, gives up the battle, returns to where his mother and grandmother are sitting, sits down, leans one elbow on the table, chin in hand, discusses something in a deep voice, self-possessed. Until, in a few minutes, he is bored again – back to the winch. The action recommences: I hear a hasty sentence terminating in the new announcement: – *AVION!* – followed by the plane's low-sweeping roar.

*

Saint-Martin-d'Albère. The trees are very green, near us, so dense that it is hard to see anything but the green leaves, the foliage, like swelling green clouds seen from above, like splashing green water. Further over there are the high mountain meadows, sloping, irregular, the rounded tops of the hills, the low mountains of Saint-Martin-d'Albère. One of the meadows is still the dark green of tall standing grass but the other has already been cut for hay and the after-grass is a light green, the green of fresh grass, and the hay has already been won and baled. The brown stone and mud of the farmhouse walls, the red tile of the roofs, the small windows in the broad walls, the second wing set at a square to the back of the house. And still further, a thousand yards or more, another farm, three buildings, same materials, same construction. Low hills crossing and recrossing, becoming bluer, and then the frontier station at the border. Then more hills, a misty dull blue-green now half enveloped in the haze and far beyond them the rising smoke and tall buildings of Ceret, a little pool of white and tile-red buildings down in the basin between the hills, the mountains. And above Ceret but separated from it by the haze and dull low cloud, hanging high above the landscape as though indifferent to it, serene, divine, the white peak of the mountain, jagged, irregular, Canigou white with snow.

The walk along Grande Randonnée 10 from Saint-Martin-d'Albère to Pic Neolous is not as interesting or as pleasant as I thought it would be. It is too steep uphill all the way and steep downhill returning, hard work going up and awkward coming back, without any proper footing. It is clear that not many people use the path for it is almost overgrown in places. And then it keeps returning to the road, crossing the road, until at last it surrenders to the road and you walk the last mile along the asphalt, hot and dull after the cool and constantly varying woods and pasture lands, and at the end of the mile of asphalt the culmination of your walk, a television relay station and some kind of ugly military installation, all barbed wire and threatening signs – *Défense de pénétrer* – *DANGER DE MORT* – sad demise from the fortresses of the past, which at least have something to admire in their architecture. It is a poor conclusion to the walk. We cannot see across into Spain but the map tells us we are right on the border. Then the path continues downhill into a dense wood full of buzzing biting insects. Where have they come from? We did not encounter any on the first part of the walk.

So we turn back, resting from time to time in the cool woodlands where the light is so filtered by the leaves or needles of the trees that it can never be hot or bright. Each tree has its own qualities. Where we enter a pine wood it is like being under water, in a cool lake, the light is soft and cool in spite of the heat and brightness of the sun, it is filtered, the bits of sun that penetrate lie scattered in soft patches without clear edges in among the luminous shade, and all the colours, the brown of the bark, the green of the needles, the tan of the dead pine needles that cover the ground, the grey of the granite rock, all are cool. But when we get to the low mountain ash the light is warm, the dead seed husks shed from the trees are brown but so near orange that they appear almost reddish and the alternating patches of reddish light and warm shadow, the bits of pink-grey stone, make a kind of camouflage, a pattern of pleasant visual confusion that keeps me from finding the red and white trail blaze until we have been sitting for a while and my eyes grow used to the effect. In spite of all the grass, and some heather, and the trees and low bushes that alternate with high mountain meadow all along the path we see no animals at all, no sheep, no cows, no goats, and except for the sound of the birds singing we are not aware of any living thing except ourselves. Of course there is often, when the wind is right, or the acoustical effect of the place we are at, the roar of the distant traffic crossing into or out of Spain, and from time to time the noise of a car following the winding road up Pic Neolous.

*

Les Sorbiers, 2 June, 8 a.m. The thick smoke spirals upward, spirals in the path of a giant corkscrew, always turning, twisting clockwise, dense white but always with darkness in it, folds, creases, bulges, dense at first near the fire and dense near the centre of the corkscrew column, rarifying then as it rises, becoming transparent at the edges, a restless continually moving changing veil of pink, white, blue. Where the fire comes from the pile of dry brush it pushes the dense yellow smoke forcefully upwards, forcefully outward, away, the smoke rises from the bottom and sides of the heap and near the top in urgent currents, joins in a central swirl, puffs and spirals away, bending before the breeze, fleeing northward when the wind blows. The sound like the sound of a soft tread, something breaking beneath a soft tread. The smell of something warm.

The spiral column of smoke rises more rapidly when the fire itself is strong, when there is a lot of dead stuff for it to burn. The fire creates the current. The fire must be strong for the smoke to push out so thickly, a thick but delicate wool, opaque, transparent. When the heap is well burnt the smoke drifts thinly away, scarcely rising, like the thin hairs of an old man, an old woman, off the black mound.

Fissier talks of the forest fire that burned out the mountain for miles around, from Banyuls to Perthus, moving at the speed of a galloping horse, leaving blackness after it.

*

The keel of the boat is long and straight, it represents the straightness of the direction the boat will go, and from it the bottom and sides spread and rise, spreading first outwards then rising upwards, a swelling, curving surface terminating in a different curve, the horizontal lines of the gun-wale, itself the upper complement of the keel below. Where does bottom end and side begin? Where middle and front? The curves are perfect in their transitions from one direction to another, their swelling fullness ever changing, never interrupted, and only the keel is straightness.

The boat is on the stone jetty and looking at the dry hull my eyes follow the diverging curving parallel lines, the curves, keenly aware of their proximity or increasing distance, the fullness, the hollowness they enclose. How has the shipwright curved the wood like that? Fitted the curving wood so closely to itself?

Near the boat a fishing-net piled in a neat round scoop, the corks lying delicately spread about the scoop, the transparency and multiple glaze of dull sea-faded colours. The flat dark pattern of irregular stone that makes the jetty is the canvas against which I see the two, net and boat.

*

2 June, Saint-Cyprien-Plage, 6 p.m., the dead gull, so long dead that he has almost become one with the sand, the sand and himself a mixture, the pale tan sand with its specks of white, grey, black, the gull himself a fading white and grey and black. Little shiny black

bugs crawl into sight from under his flattened feathers, tiny brown flies around his long still beak. His beak is long and fine and slightly parted, long and fine and gently curving, dark, and yellow only at the very tip, and his long, slender head, its black feathers in ruffled disorder, continues the direction of the beak. But below the skull the slender white neck spreads into graceful, sloping shoulders and I see how all is devoted to the wings, the delicate upper arms continuing the line of neck and shoulder down to the elbows, turning sharply upward then to the wrists, and beyond the wrists the most of the wing, the long final feathers curving at an angle down again, parallel to the sloping neck and shoulders, to the gull's sides, like long sleeves overhanging the ends of the arms. The grey body and white tail are almost lost in sand, and the grey wings, a pale faded grey, are what I mostly notice. Even within the disorder of the distintegrating feathers there is an order still, the little fine hairs of the feathers are all still running head to toe, no matter which way the limb itself seems to run the little hairs are all aligned head to toe even now to facilitate the flight through air. The wings so sharply bent at elbow and wrist must be the secret of that easy, gliding, wheeling flight, rising and falling easily, not too fast, never urgent, always searching.

*

When it is hot the oriole sings a four-note melody, the second note rising above the first, the third falling below the second and first and the final note rising again to make a lively cadence. Monsieur Fissier tells me of the farmer's interpretation of the song as saying *Ils mûriront* – 'they will ripen' – that is, the cherries. When he says the phrase his intonations sound exactly like the bird's.

His neighbours tell him he planted his radishes at the wrong phrase of the moon – *Vous n'avez pas regardé la lune*. He should have waited for the waning moon. Instead he planted them in the first quarter, which means that he will have a lot of leaf and little radish. He shrugs his shoulders. We will have to see if it is true.

*

6 June. A typical Perpignan day, bright sunlight, a breeze, warm but not too warm. But that is not what makes it typical, it is the combination of the sunlight and the breeze with the plane trees, the houses, the streets, the noise and, above all, the people. The lively walk of the people, walking rapidly, striding, passing continually, alone or two or three together, lively conversation, smiling, laughing. The leaves of the plane trees make a mottled pattern of light and shadow that the breeze modifies continually. It matches the mottled brown, tan, grey, green, yellow of the bark of the planes. People walk through the mottled light and shade and the sun highlights first one part of their bodies then another, swiftly changing, moving, the top of the head, a shoulder, a hand. Has anyone ever watched people walking through the shade of the plane trees?

The café interior is entirely covered with mirrors. There must be thirty or forty mirrors covering the different, irregular wall surfaces. Wait, I count over fifty from where I sit and there are more around the corner. The walls jut out from each other to make more surfaces for the mirrors. It is as if the designer wanted to imitate the interior of an enormous diamond cut into many facets. I order a cup of coffee and a glass of water and the waiter brings me a cup of espresso and a tiny glass of water. I think it must be bad manners to ask for free water. The mirrors are everywhere but you don't actually look in them. They are part of the decor, the backdrop. They give the impression of space. They add to the light perhaps. In their monotonous repetition they are like the unchanging rhythmic beat of the heavy music that pours from the loudspeaker of the juke-box near the door. The loudness and softness does not vary, neither does the beat : it is the repetition and the high spirits that count. The repeated images of the mirrors are like the monotonously repeating beat of the music. I am not sure which is more real, the picture in the mirror or the real people. This couple across from me become a composition in the mirrors, the composition gives them identity, it picks them out from the motley sounds and lights and movements of the café. How many times do I see them? There they are across from me not once but twice. She smiles at him, looks at her little finger. He leans over the table towards her. I see his bent back, his head hides her face but in the neighbouring image I see her face as well. Behind her, behind the image on the left, two more of her, the back of her head twice, two more of him, his face, three-quarter view and then almost full – and wait, there he is again almost in profile in a little side-mirror, and to the left there he is again, just a fragment of shoulders or a fragment of head, beside the back of her head and then her profile. So far I have seen only their reflected images, four or five of each. They talk, laugh, sip, look at each other, look away, lean heads together, smile. I turn to look at the real couple : how less real they seem ! But my eye is caught by the three more of them behind their real selves. A flash of brilliant sunlight reflected suddenly from the windscreen of a passing car flashes yellow across my open sketch-book, my writing hand. The juke-box starts a new rhythm. The girl shifts her weight and disappears from two of the three mirrors, then they both get up to study the eighty selections on the juke-box. In the mirror behind where they were sitting I see the bartender in triplicate. A sextuple waiter crosses my path of vision. I am no longer sure what is reflection and what reflected reflection. The heads of passers-by outside the café are repeated over and over again in the internal system of mirrors, made more complicated by the accidental cooperation of the café windows which catch reflections from the mirrors inside and reflect them back again. Thus that man walking towards me from the distance, outside the café, on the pavement, is actually being reflected into the mirror from the inside of the café window, the window itself having picked up the image from one of the other mirrors. I watch him approaching for a moment and then turn my head the other way – there he is, the real man, coming from a different direction altogether. His multiplied image fills the café mirror for less than a second then he passes out of sight. It is the visual equivalent of sounds echoing again and again before they die out or of thoughts endlessly repeated from one mind to the next. It reminds me that when we were in Saint-Martin-d'Albère, high in the Pyrenees, surrounded by yet higher Pyrenees, the rooster crowed again and again in response to his own repeatedly echoed voice.

*

Madame Fissier thinks that Fripon the cat has rheumatism. He limps, and snarls when she tries to pick him up, but I have seen her lift him by the front legs and I think that is the trouble. 'Kill with kindness.' He would be better if she left him alone to take his chances with the dogs, foxes, etc.

*

The owner of the little book-shop looks Catalan to me and I find him agreeable for his inefficient, unprofessional manner. I am convinced that he is more interested in matters of Catalan autonomy than in his own business. That impression is reinforced by the large number of books and pamphlets of local and Catalan interest. It is there that I find the best walking-maps of the region, the walkers guides to the local mountain trails, and so on. It is there also that I find a good selection of books by Marx and Mao Tse Tung. Look, a book by Jack London that I have never found in English! And his French accent makes it certain that he is Catalan.

Then the phone rings and I hear him unexpectedly talking Greek — fluent, perfect Greek! When he finishes his conversation we begin to talk. He has only been in Perpignan for two years. The books are only a means of making a living, not the easiest. He is continually busy, there is such a flood of new books published every day that no one can keep up with it. How does he? I ask. How does he choose what to stock?

Impossible, he says. The large distributors virtually make up his mind for him. They send him the books, which are charged directly to his bank account. If the books don't sell he has up to three months to return them. The only trouble is that it then takes six months for the distributor to return his money. Meanwhile he pays a steep interest on his overdraft. We get so engrossed in talking that he forgets the clock, then notices suddenly that it is twenty minutes past closing. He is late to pick up his son (daughter? — French does not specify) at school. He excuses himself and rushes out to push the outdoor display racks of books and postcards and maps into the shop.

In the *Monde* I notice an item about a publisher who has defaulted on the royalties due to an author whose book had run to three hundred thousand copies. The publisher's business in 1978, says the

Monde, amounted to fifteen million francs, or more than three million dollars. A group of authors have formed an organisation to try to get their money. Elsewhere in the *Monde* there is something about six hundred thousand books being published every year around the world. When I mention the figure to the Greek bookseller he says it must be an underestimate.

*

The interior of the cathedral in Perpignan is massive, solemn and dark, its vastness emphasized by the loud sounds treble and bass of the high organ. The rough edges of the high notes scrape against my ear, the vibrations of the deep ones rattle against my backbone. There is nothing in between. Outside, around the corner, down the narrow courtyard, under the high spanning arched buttresses that push the cathedral away from the opposite building, I find the simple red brick and rubble construction that we have seen in the farm houses and barns all over the Roussillon. At the end of the courtyard, tucked away as though forgotten, or meant to be forgotten, the old portal of the cathedral, white marble, relegated here now for some unknown reason, and at the centre, at the top, a stern, unusual Christ seated solemn in glory like a severe occidental Buddha, Christ the judge, leaning forward from an invisible throne, his diagonally sloping thighs, his diagonally receding shins the two sides of a triangle that the vertical folds of his robe complete. That right hand raised in a papal blessing seems to me a perfunctory concession to the obligation of mercy. It is more the left hand I see, resting solidly on the square book, the solemn set of the down-turned lips, the sternness of the neatly bearded jaw, the blank, unseeing eyes. The two frowning angels that stoop their small bodies awkwardly, rump towards heaven, to whisper in either ear are surely reciting the condemning sins, not the redeeming mercies of the accused. And from the throne on which he sits the heads and faces of two snarling dogs confirm the severity of this Christ who seems to tell us in his contained, unsmiling serenity that, with regrets, he cannot change the law. His robes swirl gracefully about his knees

78

in perfect waves and arcs, his feet grip the stone beneath his throne like hands, the toes like fingers.

*

Rue de la Marche, Perpignan :-

> *La Bourgeoisie a fait
> de la vie une
> marchandise.
> Ne mourrons pas comme les choses.*

> The middle classes
> have turned life into
> a commodity.
> Let's not die like things.

*

The cathedral at Elne is dark and cool. The heavy pilasters of the nave slant dizzily towards the right. The curve of the vault is flat as if it did not have the energy to maintain a pure arc, as if it had sagged. At the very end of the nave, above the apse, just under the flat curve of the vault, a tiny round window lets in the light. A bird flies by outside and for an instant reflects a bright flash of colour onto the vault. Someone puts a coin into the meter and the lights go on: the cool dimness is lost, and the shadows. All is reduced to plainness, flatness. I wait. Finally the lights go off, the cathedral regains its depth, its secrets. The complex pilaster-pillars model the light, the shade.

The arcades of the cloister are all bright coolness, the cloister courtyard warmth and brilliant sunlight. It is the expression of mediterranean summer. How complex this image of the creation of Eve! The marble is brown with rust and above, spanning the two columns, a multi-bodied serpent swallows a living man. The serpent's four tails issue directly from its head, twisting and twining and braiding the whole length of the lintel. The helpless mortal, disappearing legs first into the broad and yawning mouth, is passive before his fate. Below the lintel, on the capital itself, the creator god pulls the woman by her right wrist from the body of the sleep-

79

ing man. As Adam sleeps so Eve is not yet awakened, her hand hangs limp above the creative grasp, her other arm trails below, her face is dull, unseeing. Only the god is bright, alert, his look keen, his mouth alive. He bends forward, intent on his work, his shoulders hump over the lesser inert human forms, his robes swirl in living movement around his body, make elongated circles about his knees. At his head and shoulders two large and graceful geese bend their long necks to catch their padded feet in their beaks.

How like a woman this captured Christ appears! His robes are all in stormy agitation like the choppy waves of an untranquil sea. His face is flat and round, almost featureless, as one of his equally faceless captors takes him firmly by the wrists, the other by the shoulders. Here, one small step over, there is only the incised line of an eye left on the chipped face of the kneeling figure as the single tormentor swings the knout-like whip. Below the long and flowing hair – how like a woman's – above the simple skirt, the raw stripes of the whip on the bare flesh. Rounding the capital I see the other torturer, his feet apart, his weight thrown back as though in a lively dance, but above his head, ready to strike, the heavy whip, its knotted ends. And there, almost unnoticed between whipper and whipped, a divine hand descends in the two-fingered papal blessing. The Christ they lower from the T-shaped cross seems to sleep as Adam slept, his body horizontal, tranquil, his hands and arms relaxed. Only the onlookers wring their hands, caught in stiff, immobile stone. But further on all suffering is forgotten as strange faces grin, weird animals cavort.

*

8 June. The Lapidary Museum in Arles is a response to the sun, the hot bright sun of the south. Its plain stone façade seems like a surrender to the force of the sun, the continual bright shining heat of the sun. Plain pale yellow stone, as though the colour had been bleached out of it by centuries of sun, pale yellow and plain, a plain blank mass of it, the stone so smooth and flat, the light so intense, so glaring to my northern eyes, that at first I take in nothing at all. A plain façade of plain stone, it seems strange that this mass of nothing, this warehouse wall, faceless, meaningless, should be left

thus to face the splendid carvings of the portal of Saint-Trophime across the square. But the plain façade of the Lapidary Museum fascinates me, for some reason I look at it, not at Saint-Trophime. Its very plainness speaks of the place, the sun, the south. And, looking, I begin to see: the irregular sizes of the stones, as if there were a random element in the cutting of the stone, and the way the colour varies from stone to stone, more white, more yellow, some a powdery pale, almost colourless, others darker, hints of orange even, and some an astonishing faded purple red. Areas of the stone are smooth, others pitted, dark, eaten away, rotting. Looking I detect the casualness, the afterthoughts: that bit on the left was surely added later. Its newness refuses to participate – it is cooler, does not have that same burned warmth, the accumulated heat of centuries of sun, nor does it have the green tufts of grass that push out from the tight seams of the top of the façade.

Now as I look I see that even the design of the façade is not simple but oddly irregular, full of strange elements of design, two high arched windows, one to either side of the door, two narrow vertical slits, and then above the whole a narrower façade rising up to a triangular pediment flanked by its own low descending wings. On the left a strangely oriental polygonal tower, capped by a tiny dome of stone, shoulders the end of the pediment. Behind one of the wings, through that odd vertical window, I see what looks like vegetation-covered stone with the blueness of the sky above it. It gives the suggestion that there is nothing behind this great flat façade but a wild cliff, grass, brush, bushes, a shepherd perhaps and a flock of goats quietly grazing. The flatness of the pale blue sky, the pale grey of the rock, the plain darkness of the other windows, all conspire with the plain façade to make a flat design, to continue the illusion that there is nothing there, only the façade, an enormous two-dimensional drawing in stone.

But I have been inside, know better, have visited the museum, seen the ancient marbles, know the vast rectangular space. Hence the door, the portal, the oddly incongruous classic forms, relief pilasters, Corinthian capitals sculpted on the surface of the stone, classical forms so out of keeping with the provençal plainness that I did not notice them until the last. And above the portal in a little classical niche Athena, the presiding saint of this museum. Slate-grey pigeons settle in the pediment, disappear through the narrow slits, reappear

81

and fly away, swallows fly above the square but do not land. The large black doors of the museum interrupt the unity of the stone façade. They alone are out of place.

*

Two columns from the ancient Roman forum of Arles stand yet, darkened, chipped, pitted with antiquity, and a fragment of pediment above them. The whole thing is built into the hotel that faces the tiny Place du Forum. Inside, the antiquity is continued. It is a very old hotel, the proprietress is old, the furnishings are old, old in every sense : large leather armchairs, a giant blacksmith's bellows lying on its back and fitted with wrought-iron legs and so become a broad coffee-table, black marble Africans in gilded livery holding the chandeliers along the brocaded stairway, fragments of ancient sculptures embedded in the walls. There is an old-fashioned comfort to the hotel, a sense too of decay, the feeling that it cannot be kept up for long. It is the past extending briefly into the present.

Later we talk to the proprietress. She is proud of her old-style hotel, of its ancient furnishings, and also of the famous Frenchmen – poets, artists, musicians, even royalty – who have stayed in it, but proudest of all of a flag. She promises to show it to us.

The next morning we see the flag and learn its story. It is an American flag and made by hand – *fait à la main*. She tells us briefly of the hateful days of the German occupation, the welcome coming of the liberating American armies. Happy to be free, she looked for an American flag to hang out. Not surprisingly, none were to be found in the shops. Instead, she bought lengths of the tough, tightly spun and woven red, white and blue woollen cloth used in French flags, cut out the stripes and stars, stitched all together herself, hung out the flag. Later it became her custom to hang it out every Fourth of July. I notice that the stars, instead of being in the orderly eight by six arrangement that still prevailed in 1945 are scattered about, genuinely *spangled*. I notice too that the moths have been at the flag.

She explains. The flag is worn by age and is no longer in use. An American air-force general, dining at the hotel not long ago, heard the story of the flag, saw the old flag, and was so moved that he promptly sent her a new flag direct from the US air-force. The original flag became another antique.

She shows us the letter, in perfect French, that accompanied the new flag. 'Well,' she adds, 'if it were not for the Americans . . .' – *si ce n'était pas pour des Américains. . . .* She does not finish the sentence. We know what she means, and are glad that someone still has not forgotten.

*

Awakened at 6.30 a.m. by the sound of some gigantic mechanical monster, hissing and groaning, but groaning rhythmically, the rhythm of rock music against the continual hiss. It is the *tarasque*, the ancient man-devouring monster of Provence, tamed at last by Saint Martha come from Palestine to settle here, revived now in mechanical form devouring something – garbage? – waiting for a new saint to tame it again.

*

The cold grey stone of the cloister of Saint-Trophime. The morning sun bright through the arches, a woman walks along, her image flashing bright and dark in sun and shadow. Thin high double columns support tiny darkened capitals, whispered reminders of ancient stories of saints and demi-gods and gods. The stone is so grey and full of shadows that even the brilliant sunlight on the grass of the cloister courtyard seems chilled. A cypress grows, its textured vertical bark, its slanting irregular growth a reproach to the narrow straight immobility of the columns. Where once monks hauled water, poured it through pierced containers to maintain the plants and lawn of their cloister through the hot and rainless summer, the invention of a rubber tube to transport the water, of a spinning two-armed machine to spray it about, frees men for other tasks, for idleness. In place of monks tourist couples wander, restless, freed for a hasty wandering incomprehending look at the dark grey stone, the arcane chipped hard-to-perceive capitals, too darkened now with the city's life. Material here to keep eyes and mind occupied for years

83

of cloistered confinement, hard to take in anything in a few minutes, a quarter of an hour. The beardless youthful martyrs, the old nodding saints, the sacred histories. But look, there where Christ is being born, just on the other side of the narrow capital: a shepherd and his flock, and two goats reaching upward, balanced on their hind legs, to pull down toward themselves the higher branches of the tree, stretching their long necks to reach the highest, freshest leaves.

*

I sit and compare the ancient and the modern arches of the arena at Arles, asking myself whether the ancient stonework, now pitted and eroded with such long existence, was once, when it was new, as hard and sharp as the modern stone. My prejudice makes me believe that the ancient stonecutter had a softer, more feeling chisel, left the stone less impersonal, cut less to an abstract measurement, more as a form, a small form that was part of a larger form. Or is it simply the long collaboration of time? Time has cut away all detail, all preciseness of finish, all irrelevance, destroying what it could, leaving, when it left at all, only the essential forms. I admire the ancient arches of the arena, pitted, eroded, survivors – because they are *survivors* – and somehow think that had their form been less perfect, had they been conceived in less profound minds, made by less understanding, skilful hands, in forms less perfect, less meant for eternity, they would long since have crumbled, gone. And so seeing them thus I seem to see the essential, the essence of a form, the idea of arch, and see as well the long experience of time, the many risings and the many settings of the sun, the north wind, the storms of rain, the mist. The rain must wash the stone it reaches since the outsides of the arches are clean, the clean stone we see so often in Arles, but the insides are streaked with black. Pollution? It too becomes a kind of modelling, shading to express the form, or for the form to express itself.

I am only yards from the ancient arches but between me and them cars roar by, rumbling, groaning. A yellow sports car passes, its engine gunning, a fierce growl that makes my rib-cage vibrate. It is the lion's roar. I look beyond the arena to the church of Sainte-Marie, its strange agglomeration of wings stuck together at different angles, different heights, its complex bell-tower – always in this same stone of Arles – first square, then polygonal, then a tapering polygonal cone adorned with odd jutting bits of stone, as if they were left there when the stonecutter was done to serve as handholds and footholds for an ascent to the stone cross at the apex. The long wing, with its single high window, is the church but that other wing, taller, not as long, looks like a house, and there beyond the tallest wing, what is that strange low octagonal tower that is like a bit of fortress?

At intervals thudding blasts of amplified guitar and drums reach us from the ancient theatre around the corner. They are rehearsing for a rock festival. But it is only intervals of sound – the real noise will be tonight. Cars pass, then relative silence for a while. Then from within the arena, astonishingly, a loudspeaker barks commands. It sounds like a reprimand to some erring tourist. Then relative quiet. A long-haired man with a guitar sits down beside us. No amplification. The rapid soft strumming of Spanish guitar, fingers, strings. Cars pass. The music is momentarily drowned by the sound, then re-emerges. Listening, I wonder still about the ancient stonework of the arena.

Arles is a mixture of ancient and modern, side by side, compatible and yet uneasy. The ancient stone the modern stone, the roar of motors the stillness, the amplified music and barked commands the Spanish guitarist. It is the ancient things we come for.

I have written a thousand words and still not found the essential. Is it that the immobile stone is never still, that the curving arches and vaults are themselves part of a larger curve, the arches approach, recede, curving towards and away from us as we look, rising highest where they are nearest to us, descending further away as they round the curve? And always the collaboration of time.

*

Another kind of light: the Abbey of Montmajour is the other side, the reverse, of the façade of the Lapidary Museum at Arles. There all was exterior, the brilliant sun that dominated all the exterior of the building, and we were outside under the same hot, dazzling sun. Here at Montmajour we are inside and it is as if the great façade at Arles had been turned around and extended sideways into surround-

85

ing walls, upwards and over into vaulted roofs to make an enclosed space, totally enclosed by the same massive, simple walls. So simple I would like to say *impersonal*, but they are not impersonal – they are themselves – merely *simple*. And instead of brilliant light our eyes must adjust here to the dimness of the light that keeps us at first from seeing anything but the massive flatness of the walls and the high vaults, the coolness of the stone. It is the same stone – everything : walls, ceiling, floors, all in the same stone, surrounding us everywhere – but now, inside, exempt from the fierce sun and weather, it is cool, a powdery white, and yet not cool, its underlying tone is warm. But it is the protected quality I sense, the quietness appropriate to a cloister, the quietness of preservation, of thoughts of eternal things. And through the low archway of the open door, the brilliant sun seen against the darkness of the inner walls makes patterns of light and shade upon the trees, the leaves. But now it is outside, we are in.

And yet another kind of light. Unlike the cool darkness of the stone of Saint-Trophime cloister, the stone in the cloister here is warm – is it that it has been exempt from city smoke, or is there another reason for Saint-Trophime's blackness? – and the sunlight that barely sent its reflections into the arcades there here pours in from the central court, illuminates all warmly. The arcades, the vaults are warm with light and softened shadows and they are tranquil, the noisy sounds have not reached this far yet.

The ascent to the tower : a circular staircase. A hundred steps up to the little window in the stair-well. Inside, the soft light of a high room, just under the ribs of the Gothic vaulting, on the stone ledge that remains from some old, now gone joist, before the hole in the wall that is left, a pigeon, his slate-grey feathers perfect in the filtered light – the light cool luminous grey of the back and breast, the dark stripes across the tail, the greenish iridescence of the head, that almost not visible ring of purple where the dark feathers of the neck meet the light grey of chest and back. He is resting, quiet, a contrast to the restless ascending and descending of the tourists (their chirping, breathless voices), the full roundness, convexity of his form, his stillness on one leg, last remnant of the former peace of the abbey.

*

From the tower of the abbey of Montmajour you can just see Daudet's *moulin* – his windmill. It stands on a little sloping hillock of ground raised high enough above the surrounding countryside and pine woods to catch the wind which must blow fiercely off the Alpilles just to the north. We see three windmills altogether standing at a little distance from each other, each on its separate rise in the ground, but Daudet's is the only one that has been kept up. It still has a roof and the long arms of the wings, and so we can pick it out from the others. There is a bright sun and it is hot when we get there, but there is also a breeze blowing, as you would expect. The breeze makes us uncomfortable but it is what the miller wanted. It is surprisingly low, the mill, a circle of wall rising not that many yards above the rock around it and topped by a brown wooden cone of a roof. The wings are frames of wood, facing north, towards the *mistral*, the north wind, but bolted in place now and without sails. Inside, the names of all thirty-two winds are inscribed at the top of the walls just under the roof. A stuffed grey owl sits on one of the beams to remind us of the real owl that Daudet felt was also the real tenant of the mill, but we can find no sign of the rabbits. We visit the lower room, the storage room for the grain, a vault carved into the massive stone below the mill itself, the place where Daudet lived and wrote. But some say that he really lived in a comfortable château that belonged to friends and that he only went up to the mill by day.

The woman who is showing us around is anxious to close up and get to her lunch – we were late in coming – and that puts us in mind of our lunch too. Not far down the road we find the small town of Fontvieille and a tiny market just in the process of cleaning up. We are barely in time to buy some *paté de campagne* and a hunk of Swiss cheese and a long French bread and take them back up to the mill, closed up now and seemingly deserted – the best time to sit at the site of your literary pilgrimage. With the other tourists away and the guide not around to explain things to you, without the necessity to concentrate your unwilling mind on the displayed books, photos and other relics, you are free to imagine what it must have been like. What about the rabbits? Can you see any? It is the wrong time of day in any event. And those pine trees? Are they the ones he mentions at the beginning of the book? It is much the way he describes it. But what about that town down there, Fontvieille? Could it have been as large as that in Daudet's time? Not likely. It was much smaller and everything was even more rustic than it still appears even today. And the distant hum of the few cars that have not stopped for lunch – that was never there. Oxen pulled the carts and ploughs and horses the wagons and coaches that Daudet describes.

The breeze makes our picnic awkward. On a site meant to catch the wind it is hard to get away from the wind. Still it would not do to eat anywhere but at the mill. We sit on a huge round millstone left just beside the walls, high enough and broad enough to be both chairs and table, taking in the landscape while we eat the *paté* and cheese and bread. For a few moments a cloud covers the sun, then disappears. Seeing the landscape in both sun and cloud we know that it is true what he says, that the south lives by its sun. The sun makes everything live.

*

It is Sunday when we go to the abandoned chapel of Saint-Gabriel. We pass groups of cyclists in uniform red and blue jerseys and caps embroidered with the name of the business enterprises that are sponsoring them. We get to the chapel, set back from the road at the top of a flight of steps, just as a group of hikers with packs are going beyond the red and white blaze on an olive tree that is beside the trail. France is taking advantage of its Sunday for a little recreation and exercise.

Above the door of the chapel Adam and Eve stand with their serpent and beside them Daniel with his two lions, and above them all the archangel is carrying Habakkuk, with a firm grip on his hair, to bring a loaf of bread to Daniel. While we are looking and expressing our admiration two young men rush up from the road. They are in a hurry and semi-breathless. They show us photographs of relief carvings and ask if we know where the reliefs are to be found. Have we seen them? They notice Satia's book on the Romanesque art of Provence and start to flip through the pages eagerly. I tell them that they will not find their reliefs in the book, since the book is only Romanesque (and – what I neglect to say – their reliefs are not) but they continue thumbing, thinking they have caught a glimpse of what they wanted and then going back to try to find the page. I repeat that the book is only Romanesque, but still with no effect. I say it a third time, and finally the message penetrates. One of the young men realizes that what they are looking for is not Romanesque, therefore cannot be in the book he is flipping through. The way he expresses this realization is by repeating what I have said, not about his photos, but about the book: *Ah, ce n'est QUE roman . . . !*

I ask him why they are so anxious to find the reliefs. They look embarrassed. Clearly the explanation will be too time-consuming. *C'est un jeu,* one of them explains – a game – and, thanking us courteously, they rush away down the steps and back to their car. As they go I notice clumps of cyclists in uniform jerseys and caps gliding rapidly past along the road, accompanied by the sound of many cars whose motors are gunning, anxious to get where they are going this Sunday. Around us olive trees and fig trees and the sound of many birds.

*

Hot day in Avignon. Thin clouds, dull sun, heat, buzzing motor-bikes, too many cars. The French are voting for Europe today. We see the neatly dressed elderly couples entering and leaving the polling stations. At noon all shops close. To the bridge. THE bridge. *Le pont d'Avignon.*

No dancers. I find a place to sit, a kind of bulk of stone set into the corner of the city walls just where the street comes through them, and sit down to admire the three remaining graceful low arches that extend into the Rhone towards the 'new' city on the other side. Then I notice: from where I sit a big red STOP sign is smack between me and the bridge. Right in the line of sight. I am too fatigued by the heat to get up. Instead I look at the other tourists. A car pulls up and parks in a little dusty central island of the boule-vard. A first-communion girl, in the white habit of a convent novice, stands to have her picture taken in front of the bridge. All the family are dressed up, full of good spirits. Almost at once another car, another girl in the white novice habit. And another. One after the other in front of the bridge. It must be the thing to do. The first-communion picture before the bridge. When Satia tells me that what we are looking at is not the original bridge I vaguely remember having heard that before. But I had forgotten it. All I remembered was sitting on the grass on that long island in the middle of the river and looking across at the romantic ruined arches of the Pont d'Avignon, where people once danced. A French farmer happened by while I was sitting there and we chattered – in so far as we could, me with my poor French and him with his *langue d'oc* to make my comprehension even more limited. Now there is a wire fence stretched along the riverfront and a campsite behind it. No use even trying to pay a nostalgic visit today. Besides, Satia adds, they did not dance on the bridge but under it.

Back at the palace of the popes, sitting on the ground at one corner of the vast square and leaning against the low wall, a young man and a young woman play their flutes. Seventeenth-century duets float into the air, rise and fall in the graceful rhythmical dance-steps of another time. It is the dance heard, no longer seen. Duet follows duet. Between each piece he mops the sweat from his face. Coins clink into the little basket they have put down in front of them as they clinked once in the indulgence boxes of the popes. People are clearly grateful for the music. So are we and we sit on the steps nearby and listen until at last he mops his face for the last time, then mops the moisture out of his flute. She does the same and they pack up, count their coins and leave. In front of us a little terrier on a leash, tongue hanging out, panting desperately, tries to crawl into a bit of shade cast by the wall. His mistress pulls him after her, not noticing his distress.

We go into the Petit Palais to see the long long series of Italian primitives newly displayed there. The continual buzz of some machine – air conditioning? fluorescent lighting? – is a source of barely perceived distraction. Outside the light is rich and brilliant but they have carefully screened it out and lighted the pictures artificially, fluorescent lights and harsh spotlights. It makes the paintings monotonous, opaque, unfeeling. The buzzing and the harsh lighting are tiresome. At last we reach a room where the lights are off and the pictures become themselves. Scarcely aware of the difference I begin to look at the paintings with pleasure. The guard, an old man, dozes heavily in his chair near the door. His back is curved forward and his head is on his chest. For a moment he seems to waken and look at me with wide-open suspicious eyes. Then at once he sleeps again.

He stirs in his sleep and expresses some deep anguish in a restless phrase. We continue looking at the paintings. He wakes up, gets out of his chair, makes a circuit of his little domain of three rooms. It is then that I notice the lights are off in all three of the rooms. We conclude that it is the guard who turned them off. Not to disturb his nap? Or does he too prefer the natural light? His clothes are old and poorly kept. He has not shaved today. He mutters some personal grief to himself and goes back to his chair. I know how he feels. In his shoes I would do the same: turn off the lights, let my clothes go to hell, forget to shave, disintegrate under the monotonous solitary confinement of the watcher of the lovers of art who cannot be trusted with the art they love.

*

The drunken farmer in Avignon, his red smiling clown-like face. He is like a Donegal hill farmer in for polling-day. All over the EEC the farmers are in to vote. Are the politicians paying for their transportation and giving them plenty of free drinks everywhere?

The way he is dressed. The cheap brown Sunday shoes, not very expensive but not very worn either. He wears a sturdier kind of shoe most of the time. His slightly yellowed white cotton shirt, the sleeves too long: quality cotton coloured with age. The right cuff of the shirt sticks out of the jacket sleeve. A black tie of an old-fashioned cut that is several inches too short to reach his belt. The plain grey trousers are also too short and too full in the seat, ultra roomy. Not very stylish but easier to move about in, work in. Over the white shirt a grey cardigan, open, just visible under the old brown tweed jacket. And the beret worn just like an Irish tweed cap, not pushed over to one side. He comes along and does a little dance, sings a bawdy song. His face could be an Irish face. Is it because he is a peasant farmer? Or is it the Celtic strain? I think of Ireland and wonder if he gets drunk half a dozen times a year perhaps, the rest of the time tied to the farm, the work, the old father and mother, too shy to approach a woman, living a long bachelorhood. Then a day in town, plenty to drink. Off to do a little dance, sing a little snatch of bawdy song. Satia says he is like a puppy looking for a friend. None of us want to have anything to do with him. He crosses the street and brings the rushing cars to sudden halts, majestic in spite of his wobbly step. The tourists are amused but the French are annoyed.

*

Sunday, 10 June, afternoon. At Glanum we sit around, scores of us, or hundreds, on the old stones, and look at or draw or paint the crumbling Roman arch, the ancient funerary monument. We eat peaches at five francs a box sold from a van by a drowsing Algerian who wakes up the instant my eye falls on the peaches. My first look at the monument was a surprise. I thought it was a World War One monument, something from the twenties or thirties. But it was a little rough and crumbly for that. The guide book says it is the best preserved of Roman monuments. It makes me realize how faithfully they were still copying ancient styles only fifty years ago.

Looking more closely at the sculpted scenes of battle that emerge from all four sides, I see how they are crumbling. Their state, seen close up, is worthy of their age. And how vivid! Faces gone, arms and legs decaying, they are still like living men, living horses and dogs intent on their inevitable, clamorous battle. Here is a warrior whose battleaxe is only an incised outline, the arm that raises it little more than that, his face a blur on the remaining roundness of his head. This other one, before him, leaning backwards once for some battle purpose – to increase the force of the blow, perhaps – seems now to be falling helplessly, his legs and buttocks melted away, his backbone gone, his flesh flowing from him. The dog that squatted at his feet is only a bit of body now. At the other end of the scene a horse rears up, its legs and snout gone. It is a horse yet in spite of its losses. And in the centre of the composition, that figure who seems to recline, is he wounded, dying? Other figures lean towards him in dismay. A final word? A last embrace? Whatever he was doing once, living or dying, he is dying now, disappearing as the marble that is his self distintegrates, nothing more now than an almost formless, liquid shape. Just recognizable. The last instant before the soul flies wailing off to hell. The effect is different where the stone retains its hard grey patina splattered with white and yellow lichen, but here the stone is flesh-coloured, seems alive, subject to death.

The figures, so alive in their long battle, seem not merely to erode but to die slow crumb of stone by crumb of stone. And above, that long wreath of leaves, those grotesque satyr masks, like masks of ancient comedy, sardonic, seem to say this is only a scene that soon will end. All will pass away, even the figures in the stone.

*

Arles, Hôtel de Ville, Sunday night. They are counting the votes at city hall. At a long table three people sit, or stand, open grey-blue envelopes, take out a printed ballot, hand it to the referee. The ballots are not marked – any mark invalidates them – the voter has merely chosen the list he wants and put that printed list in the blue-grey envelope. There are separate printed ballots for every list.

As they hand the ballots to him the referee reads out the ballot, announcing the choice not according to the party name printed on the list of candidates but according to the name of the politician who heads the list. *Veil*, for instance for the government list, *Mitterand* for the socialists, *Marchais* for the communists. As he calls out the name he sticks the ballot onto a tall spike, the kind small business men use to keep their bills and receipts, a separate spike for each of the nine parties. Four people sit at another long table, before them large sheets covered with small squares printed in light brown ink, ball-point pens in their hands. As the votes are called off they mark one side of a square that is opposite the name of the candidate. When the four sides of the square are full and the name is called a fifth time they make a diagonal line across the square and call out *cinq*. Each person is recording four or five parties so that there are two records of every ballot and two people call out *cinq* each time, thus confirming each other's count. The referee has stuck the five ballots on to the spike near the top, without pushing them down, and when he hears the recorders call out *cinq* he re-counts those five ballots and then presses them tightly down on to the ones already at the bottom of the spike, and the count up to five begins again. Thus they have a triple control of the count.

Outside in the entrance hall a large bulletin board has been set up, a small crowd of men and women has gathered. The results are being written up. By midnight, fifteen of the thirty-one districts are in.

Thirteen of the fifteen have gone heavily communist. But that is no surprise since the communists, it is said, are always strong around Arles and Marseilles.

*

Beaucaire. The Rhône flowing slowly, Tarascon and its château and church across the river, the flat landscape : distant low hazy hills of the Alpilles, the dark hedgerows of cypresses and other trees, the middle ground of yellow ripening grain, the foreground green – fresh grass, fresh bamboo.

Beaucaire : ancient city – the fairs – the bulls – walls, ramparts – the castle now a vast unkempt park – the wild growth of trees – the young guard – the small chapel with old bits of catapults, cannon balls, stones – the triangular tower.

It is late when we arrive at the gate to Beaucaire château, we have been driving most of the day and we are tired. The castle ruins are high above us on a hill. We were able to see them from a distance but once in the town itself we quickly get lost in the short, narrow, curving streets. The high walls of the old buildings rising close to one another block our view to the castle and we lose our way at once. People look at us curiously as I try to manoeuvre our car past other cars or vans coming out of even narrower side streets. We have the sense of being out of place, of ignoring unseen 'No Entry' signs that everyone else is aware of. We drive into a tiny square and women sitting with long-haired, long-bearded young men at a pavement café look up in amusement, derision. There is no feasible way out of the square but to drive around it and out through a set of low stone arches. In time we find ourselves back at the city wall at the very gate we entered by.

This time we try a different route but somehow get involved in the same confusing system of narrow, inevitable streets, the constant risk of scraping another car or even a cornerstone. The same tiny square again, the same young women and long-haired, long-bearded bohemians, the same looks. The same arches again.

Finally we do get to the gate of the castle and I park the car. Above us the castle stands high on a rough hill. Even the iron gate to the enclosure is thirty good steps above the level of the street. It is late in the afternoon and we have been driving all day and Satia decides to stay in the car, for she is tired, but I do not want to pass up what may be my only chance to see the old castle. I count the steps as I go up and find that they divide roughly into two groups, the first of eighty, the second of eighty-one. It is hard to count exactly — the ground is rough, many of the old steps are only slanting ramp-like stretches of gravelly earth. Once past the high iron gate it is like a vast uneven park without keepers. Trees and bushes grow wild and at random, tall grass, dirt paths with stones lying about, crooked uneven ascents, broken remnants of the steps, weeds and wild flowers in disarray. Nothing here has been planted, everything has planted itself, wildly, naturally. On old stone benches or folding chairs women sit, some with their children, some with pet dogs, some knitting, talking among themselves in little groups.

Half-way up to the castle itself there is a small office and a hand-lettered semi-official looking sign about the visit to the château, but the office is locked and no one is inside. At that point the path turns sharply to the left and the second eighty-one steps mount unevenly through trees and flowering bushes. Just before I reach the stone gate of the inner enclosure I catch sight of the Rhône below me and on my right, with a view of the castle of Tarascon on the opposite bank.

Inside the gate and to the right two people are sitting on a rough stone bench — the warm yellow stone that is everywhere in this region — talking. The young woman, dark complexioned, full-bodied, colourfully dressed, so that she seems a gypsy, is knitting rapidly, talking as she knits. The young man beside her is in uniform, I vaguely recognize the dress-uniform of the French army, the flat cylinder and large peak of the cap, the neat jacket-like blouse buttoned straight down the front, the perfectly creased trousers and highly polished leather shoes. But as he sees me and breaks off the conversation with the young woman and rises from the bench, I notice that the shoes are in fact the bulky made-to-order boots of a cripple and that he is raising himself only with effort, his weight on a cane I had not noticed before, pushing himself up as much by the strength of his right arm as by the power of his legs. He walks towards me, a certain difficulty in his step, using the cane. Locks

95

of dark-black hair that have escaped from the neat cylinder of the cap frame his head, accentuating the clear handsome face and eyes that now are looking at mine. He asks if I would like a tour of the castle. In fact I would not, I would prefer to be left alone to wander around, but I see no way to refuse the tour and I put my hand into my jacket pocket to find change for the ticket — touring about has conditioned me to be prepared to pay for every such service — but instead of selling me a ticket the guard asks me to follow him, turns away, and leads me to a small stone chapel near where we have been standing. The chapel has been turned into a little museum with old cannons and stone or iron cannon balls, old catapults, bits of weaponry. I sit on a wooden bench before these displayed objects and listen to the guard's detailed explanation. While I sit he remains standing, in spite of the difficulty and with an effort, supporting himself on his cane as he speaks. He gives a brief account of the castle, setting its existence into its historical context, and then goes on to discuss the cannons and cannon balls and other remnants of early artillery. He talks slowly and very clearly so that I can easily follow everything he is saying, understand every word, but I sense, or think I sense, the impediment in his speech that matches the impediment in his walk. If he does not stumble in either it is because of the effort, the discipline.

I listen carefully to the intricate details of history and archaeology he lays before me, struck by the almost scholarly nature of his discourse. From time to time he pauses and questions his own words. *Some say*, he points out, *that we should date this to such and such a century, but in my opinion* ... and then he goes on to give his own views and his own reasons. It all has an impressive, erudite sound.

Therefore I give him my most serious attention, wondering at this show of scholarship. He is only parroting, I think, the words of some learned professor he has heard conducting people through these ruins. The guards and guides I have encountered are not given to thinking out the histories and qualities of the objects they guard and explain. The best of them repeat their talks so exactly word for word, the intonations themselves and even the little witticisms so exactly repeated from one tour to the next that I have found following them around two or three times a good way to learn French. In short, I am more amused by this guard's learning than impressed by it.

What I am impressed by is the effort, the effort to hold himself erect, standing in spite of the difficulty his legs and feet give him, and also the effort by which he enunciates so clearly the words he is speaking, and so I give him my full attention.

The talk concluded he leads me from the chapel past the still knitting young woman and in the direction of the high tower that is, along with the walls, the only other surviving building of the old château. It is neither round nor square but triangular and that gives it an odd, striking effect. We are on the highest level now of this rough park, uneven dusty ground with scattered bushes and tufts of grass, weeds and wild flowers growing up among the fallen stones and pitted excavations of the ruins. We pass the stone wellhead of the old cistern. Two wooden benches are set at the edge of the plateau facing the red-tiled roofscape of Beaucaire with its cathedral rising above it. I adjust my step to the guard's and we progress slowly towards the tower, which is topped by elegant overhanging crenellations. In the hundred yards or so of our walk we leave history aside and begin to chat instead. He asks where I am from and learning that I am, as he had thought, American he talks about the final days of the last war, the final American bombings of the German occupying force. The vividness of his description surprises me, for he looks too young to have witnessed it himself. He sees my surprise and quickly explains that he has heard all this from his father, that he himself was born only two years after the war, in 1947. He is thirty-two.

We reach the high triangular tower. A few stone steps lead up to the wooden door. Seating himself wearily on the third step from the ground the guard explains in his clear, simple French that he is not able to make the ascent with me, and he invites me to go up on my own. He adds that he would be grateful to me if I would let him know if I find anyone else in the tower, for it will soon be time for him to close the château grounds and he is not allowed to leave anyone behind.

The tower steps are narrow and hollowed by use and I climb them slowly, cautiously keeping my footing. There are only two high arching rooms, one above the other, with the usual soft sound of pigeons nesting, and then I reach the high flat roof. When I go to the edge to look out across the crenellations at Beaucaire's roofs and river and Tarascon and the fields of Languedoc and Provence I realize that the edges of the roof have been built out from the rest of the tower and that I am standing three or four feet beyond the walls of the tower itself looking straight down on the high ground, the steps where the guard is still sitting. Open spaces that have been left in the floor of this balcony-like extension make the sensation of height and emptiness even sharper. On the other side of the roof the ground is twice as far away, for that side of the tower has been built sheer with the outer wall of the enclosure, and I am looking down hundreds of feet on to the passing traffic. I begin to wonder about the trustworthiness of the old tower roof. In spite of the massiveness of the stones I have a sense of the empty space beneath me and my legs tingle as I look down.

Thus physically aware of the height of the tower from the top I make my cautious way downward again along the narrow, hollow winding stone steps. Outside, the young woman, still knitting, is standing talking to the guard. I do not understand any of their talk but there is something serious about it. As I come down the last few steps the guard breaks off the conversation and turns to me. We talk briefly about the tower. Noticing a stone embedded in the wall near the door and inscribed with some words in a dialect I do not understand, I ask him about it. He tells me it is in languedoc. I ask him if he understands that language and he replies that he speaks it badly. To speak it well it would be necessary to associate with the old people of the region, those – of whom only a few are left – who spoke it in their youth. He goes on to say that he, like all young people today, has little to do with the old, and he explains that the old have no patience with the young of the present time, since the young are lazy, hate work, and are given to all kinds of worthless amusement. It is clear that the guard's sympathies are not with his own contemporaries, but our conversation is broken off at that point by the urgent interruption of the young woman, who is eager to continue her own conversation, or else to protect the young man from the fatigue which shows on his face. The guard points out a short route back to the main gate and I say goodbye to them both.

Some time elapses before we are in Beaucaire again but the château and the guard have remained in my mind. This time both Satia and I make the climb up the one hundred and eighty-one steps through the unkempt park to the castle. Because I had remembered the guard in conversation with the young woman I am surprised to find him sitting alone on the yellow stone bench, leaning back against the wall, his cylindrical cap pushed back on his head, his heavy stick leaning against his knees. On seeing us he adjusts his cap and rises, as before pushing himself upward with the stick. The first few words are like those of the previous visit and I can tell at once that he does not remember my having been there. We go to the chapel and he begins his explanation. To my surprise it is not the same as the previous one. He has perceived that Satia speaks and understands French well and although I only nod in agreement with what is being said he assumes the same for me. Therefore he speaks more rapidly and includes a good deal more than he did before. Though he is speaking more rapidly it is still slow enough and clear enough for me to follow. He pauses for questions, and each question that Satia asks leads him to new aspects of the castle's history and its place in the history of Languedoc, of France. All the while we are sitting on the wooden bench he remains standing, supporting himself with effort on his cane.

The talk finished we walk to the triangular tower, as before passing the roofs of Beaucaire laid out below us to our left. It is nearly noon, the sun is high, and in the warmth and intense southern light the old scattered stones and semi-excavated ruins remind us of other ruins we have seen, remains of ancient Greece and Rome. The high park is deserted, the benches empty, and we get a sense of what those other places must have been before the crowds came to fill them with their continuous shuffling, peering, photographing movement – as they were when they could be seen, felt. The guard senses our appreciation of the place and continues to talk about Beaucaire. At the tower he again asks me to let him know whether there is anyone inside, for it is time for the midday two-hour closing of the castle grounds. He points out that the lock of the tower door has been broken by vandals and therefore the tower is always open and anyone can slip in without his knowledge. He has sent for the locksmith, who has promised to repair the lock soon.

After our visit to the tower the three of us walk slowly back to the stone gate near which the guard was sitting when we came up, our pace matching his as we go. At the gate he pauses and puts a whistle to his mouth. Drawing himself up and filling his lungs he blows a shrill blast, and another, and then, with an obvious effort that distorts his features and reddens his face, he cries out twice in a loud voice that the château is closing and that everyone must leave until two o'clock. When we have descended the upper eighty-one steps and are on the lower level of the château grounds he pauses again, repeats the whistle and the announcement. We are so used to loudspeakers everywhere we go that this unexpected use of the human voice in the way it was once used startles us and seems strange, another echo of the past.

Suddenly the sound of a jet fills the air, grows louder, becomes intense, and a Mirage fighter passes quickly overhead, so low that we can easily see the bombs attached to its wings, its sound interrupting our talk, our heads turning upwards instead. As the sound subsides we resume our talk but in a moment the jet is back overhead, speeding in the other direction. This time the guard sees our puzzlement at this low, menacing flight. We wonder why it is necessary for a French jet to buzz French territory. He tells us that there are always jet fighters aloft with atomic bombs slung under their wings. They are for retaliation in case of enemy attack. This leads him to mention the super-missile the US is said to be developing. 'Why?' he asks. 'What use can it be put to?' – *A quoi utile?* – but the last few minutes of the conversation become strangely philosophical rather than political.

The following afternoon we are back again, feeling somehow that we have not yet completed the visit. There are a few tourists wandering around as though without purpose but we do not see the guard. Near the tower there are some large blocks of stone just the right size for seats and we sit on them and talk about the ruins, the traces of buildings that are no longer there, the wild flowers and the weeds and grass, and the cistern that still stands in the middle of the park, speculating on how many gallons of water it held, how long that amount would last a garrison. Finally we hear the guard's voice. He is walking slowly up from the lower park talking to some tourists who are with him. Evidently they are French for he is talking rapidly, engrossed in some explanation, clarifying some detail. He leads them to the tower door. As they go in he turns and notices us.

His smile indicates that he is glad we have returned and he comes over and greets us. He intends to join us on our informal perches. Seeing him look around for a place to sit I get up to offer him mine, but he refuses politely and chooses the nearest suitable stone, a low rounded one that looks uncomfortable and awkward. He settles down on to it easily, losing none of the dignity that goes with his neat tan uniform and cap. Resting his cane against his knees he asks us how we have been spending our time. We recount the various places we have visited in twenty-four hours and again the conversation turns to history. This time the guard goes into the history of the town and region in much greater detail than before, and kings and battles and dates and historical circumstances follow one another in profusion. I concentrate on what he is saying but I realize that I will remember little. My American mind is not used to the multiple complexities of European history, trained instead to think of history as originating in 1492, progressing through 1609 to 1776 and then on to a relatively short series of elective rulers whose reigns were finite terms of four-year periods, hence easily recallable. When the guard finishes what he is saying I remark on this contrast of European and American history, the length and complexity of the one, the brevity and relative simplicity of the other. At once he reminds me that America had a history long before 1492, and he begins to talk of the Indians of the two Americas with more knowledge than I could do. I make some remark to the effect that he has taught me a lesson even in my own country's history. The guard declines the implied compliment but begins to talk about himself none the less, about his own schooling and his passion for history to the exclusion of all other subjects, so that while he read many volumes of history he was not required to, he could not be persuaded to study mathematics. Now, he adds, he regrets his early obstinacy, for had he applied himself to his studies he could have done much more with his life, much more than being a lonely guard in the almost deserted ruins of Beaucaire castle.

Another small group of tourists is approaching from the direction of the old chapel. Seeing them the guard leans forward to rise, but as he puts his weight on his stick he loses his balance, deceived, evidently, by the lowness of his seat and, half erect but half sitting still, somewhere between the two, he rolls semi-crouched slowly and easily forward, seems to leave the ground with his feet while floating towards it with his head. The approaching tourists start over to help him, as do the French couple, who have emerged from the tower just in time to see the guard's involuntary somersaulting fall. I am nearest to him and offer my hand to help him up, but he does not need help and instead pushes himself up from the ground with the help only of his cane. His cap is lying on the ground still and his dark-black hair is scattered in locks about his face. I retrieve the cap and try to brush the dust, of which he has picked up surprisingly little, from his jacket. Even more surprisingly, he does not appear to have hurt himself. He smiles and assures us that it is not the first such fall. 'I am used to them,' he adds, and quickly turns his attention to the other tourists, sending the new ones up into the tower and offering to guide the French couple through the exhibits of the old chapel. They have been so impressed by the fall that they decline his offer hastily and the guard turns back to talk to us. In answer to Satia's questions he tells us of an old stone relief we can see in the cathedral, on one of the walls, and we assure him we will not fail to look for it. When the last group of tourists comes out of the tower he goes off with them towards the chapel and we watch his slow, difficult walk. As we descend towards the street we are aware, from what he has said, of his loneliness, his sense of frustration, but we are sorry to leave the world of thought he has created in his loneliness among the ruins of the old castle.

The cathedral is only a hundred yards or so away and we find it easily and look for the relief, but it is nowhere inside. I ask a group of teenage boys and girls. They look blank. An old woman, and she thinks for a long while, then directs me to another church. Satia comes around a corner of the building. She has found the relief high up on the south wall. We stand in the narrow lane and tilt our heads back, looking upward as if to the sky. There it is, forty feet up perhaps, or fifty, protected from the world and almost from our view by the buildings across from it on the other side of the narrow lane. Only where a narrow side-street goes off can we move back and observe it more comfortably. The final events in the life of Christ move from left to right, small figures in white stone acting out events seen so often in art that no one now will take the trouble to crane his neck to see them yet once more, so high up, saved that way from the vandalism that has ruined so much else, solitary in their height.

*

Graveson : early afternoon. We notice that the church sun-dial reads 1.15 when the clock says 3.15. There were no time-zones in those days, so the clocks conformed to the sun. Then the clocks were made to conform to time-zones, then put an hour ahead for daylight saving time. Satia complains that it is still hot at 5 o'clock, but I remind her that it is only 3.00. When we go in for lunch at 12 noon it is really only 10.00 in the morning. It is all mixed up.

*

Boulbon : old southern town, narrow streets, church. A worn low relief of a *chrism* – a cross in a circle – a hand, a lamb, all hardly noticeable thirty feet up on the wall of rubble and clay.

*

My curiosity about the great and famous Rabelais is too strong for me and I buy a paperback copy of *Gargantua*, even though I know I will not be able to understand Rabelais's archaic French. I leave the fresh, new book on the bed-side table in our room at the Hôtel Nord-Pinus. Though I am tired when we get back from a day of sight-seeing, curiosity impels me to take a quick look at the new volume before turning off the light. Rabelais's prose is too difficult for the late hour so I turn to the editor's introduction instead.

As I read, expecting the dry prose of scholarship, I am amazed instead by the richness of the editor's style, by the depth of his view of the world and of literature, by the fullness of his appreciation of Rabelais the genius, and – most of all perhaps – by the boldness and daring of his assertions.

'The world as stomach.' That, he tells us, is Rabelais. He expands upon the theme. There are three focal points within each of us : brain, heart, stomach, the first for thought, the second for love, the third for begetting. The stomach – the guts – can lead to heroism, but also to corruption. 'The intestines readily become entrails.' (I wonder, as I read, how any scholar can allow himself such bold unpedantic thoughts, but I am delighted.) What is the stomach – the material man – without the thinker? 'When Diogenes disappears, nothing is left but the cask.' Rabelais, doctor and priest, found his world, the world of the sixteenth century, in precisely that condition: 'Henry the Eighth a vast paunch, Rome an old woman stuffed to the gills. Rabelais regarded the situation, shook his head, burst into laughter. . . . While Luther sermonized, Rabelais mocked, enthroning a dynasty of bellies, creating a farce of giants.'

With each new phrase I feel myself growing more enthusiastic. It is late, the city is asleep, there is silence and I am in a cosy bed, reading. In the darkness the lamp behind me and over my head casts an intimate, isolating light on to my book. There is something, possibly, intoxicating about the situation, for I am frankly intoxicated by the grand prose of this unknown (to me at least) literary critic. Then, when I have read through the four pages of the introduction, I come upon the signature of their author . . . Victor Hugo. It is the first time I have ever read any of this great man's writing and as I turn off the light I am thoroughly under his influence.

In the morning I notice that this introduction to Rabelais is in fact an extract from a larger work, an *Essay on William Shakespeare*. That is even more intriguing. What was Victor Hugo, a French novelist, doing writing about Shakespeare? And where did Rabelais come in?

I decide to track down this new work, and I go to a serious bookshop in Perpignan, one I have visited before, to ask for it. The owner, a man in young middle-age (or perhaps what Rabelais himself would call 'a green old age') looks at me solemnly for a moment. He has seen me before, he knows I buy books in French from time to time, but now, clearly, he is sizing me up. Not flippantly, but seriously. There is a question in his mind. I think I know what it is: he cannot quite decide whether I am English or American (for Ireland does not occur to him, although it is Ireland that has played havoc with my American accent). He is also trying to hide his incredulity. It has something to do with the egotism of the English (he is thinking), supposing that the great French novelist Victor Hugo would spare time from his great fiction and poetry to write an essay on the Englishman William Shakespeare.

His incredulity gradually becomes more apparent and he asks me to repeat the author and the title. More incredulity. He has never heard of such a work, he says. Am I sure it exists? He certainly does not have it in stock. Where have I heard of it?

I have read an excerpt from it, I declare, in a paperback of Rabelais. More incredulity. The crudeness of my French and the thickness of my accent hardly go with the reading of the difficult prose of Rabelais. He rushes out from behind the counter to search the paperback shelves. The volume of Rabelais in question is not there. *Impasse.*

Then he remembers the catalogue of books in print. In France that catalogue is not a huge, heavy red volume but a series of microfilm sheets. He flicks on his viewing-machine, finds the right piece of celluloid, focuses, dials around, and then, with astonishment :-

Vous avez raison! – 'You are right!'

Such a work does exist, is actually in print. Smiling but baffled, he apologizes. Apologizes, that is, for the implied insult, the suggestion of my ignorance, an insult which I myself had not perceived, certainly not taken offence at.

Victor Hugo's *Essay on William Shakespeare* is virtually unknown in France but finally I locate a copy in the Perpignan library. To my surprise it fills a large volume, four hundred pages. If it is an essay, it is a massive one. I have no hope of reading it, the best I can do is flip through, skim it for gems, taste the richness of its prose for an hour or two. It ranges over all literature, and it is full of flashes of insight like the ones I have found in the Rabelais introduction. If I try to absorb too many I will forget all. I decide to choose one, one short phrase to remember. It is a passage where Victor Hugo is talking about grandeur and simplicity, in the world and in poetry. They are not incompatible, he says. On the contrary, simplicity is appropriate to grandeur. He gives an example. 'The sun,' he says, 'is simple' – *Le soleil est simple.* I find the words their own best demonstration. Simplicity and grandeur! How much they say about Victor Hugo, more even, perhaps, than about William Shakespeare.

*

Back page of the *Monde*, 16 June : 'GRENOBLE : THE PRESIDENT-DIRECTOR-GENERAL OF A COMPANY DISAPPEARS LEAVING A "HOLE" OF 40 MILLIONS' – The head of a company that makes women's clothing goes off with forty million francs – better than nine million dollars. The workers have not been paid since April.

On the same back page : 'BEATEN BY HER FATHER, MURDERESS AT THIRTEEN AND A HALF.' That tells the whole thing. The mother committed suicide six years ago. The father was given to drink and burglary. After a particularly bad beating the girl took her father's own carbine and, while he was sound asleep, shot him point-blank in the head, then went and told a neighbour what she had done. As this is France she has the possibility of comprehending justice.

*

Sunday, 17 June. *Cargolade* with the Fissiers. The Fissiers have invited us for a *cargolade*. Therefore instead of going to Collioure for the market we stay home. I go into town to buy a loaf of bread and a newspaper, and Madame Fissier asks me to get her a loaf of bread too. It is the occasion for a pleasant conversation : which baker she prefers (long discussion of the geography of Argeles, which is simple enough, but I am not up on the terminology and do not know any street names), exactly how am I to tell the woman what kind of bread I want (that turns out to be amazingly simple : *un gros pain, bien cuit* – a large bread, well done), with much discussion about which parking-lot I am going to leave the car in, and so on.

The *cargolade* begins about noon. It is supposed to be out of doors – a picnic – but there is too much wind, the *tramontane* is blowing. Once it starts it goes on for three days at least, and if it does not stop then it will go on for three more days, and so on by multiples of three : three, six, nine, twelve. Always by multiples of three. So we have the *cargolade* in the living room instead, which I find just as nice, with the bright Mediterranean light pouring in through the large doors. *Apéritif.* Small crackers. Grilled snails – *escargots*, whence the name *cargolade* – with *aïoli*, the garlic mayonnaise that must always be home-made – in this case, for this area, it is always made by the one particular neighbour who is most expert – grilled sausage, grilled lamb-chops, plenty of red wine. That is the picnic. Madame Fissier begins to sing somewhere between the snails and the sausage, beautiful French melodies. More and more good cheer. About three-thirty off we go to Banyuls for coffee, ice-cream, cake in a sea-side café. Then back again and upstairs to listen to some records. Monsieur Fissier puts on nostalgic French songs of the end of the nineteenth century, then *musique folkloristique d'Alsace*. To me it sounds incredibly Teutonic. While it is on Madame Fissier shows Satia a long series of family and wedding photographs. Listening to the music I get up and look over their shoulders. It seems like a strange moment to me. This Germanic music, these faces of young French men and women, the constant menace of invasion and death from a more warlike neighbour that has hung over them for so long, the number of photographs I have seen of young Frenchmen dead in war against the Germans. For a moment a kind of confusion invades my brain : these are the pictures of living young French men and women, but will I some day be looking at them as pictures of the dead, dead in another war? The music plays. It is no wonder Madame Fissier remarked after the meal, when we were all in a terribly good mood : *Voilà un autre repas que les prussiens n'auront pas* – 'One more meal the invaders won't get.'

*

At the café Monsieur Fissier tells us this verbal puzzle :
> *Si six scies scient six cigares*
> *six cent six scies scient six cent six cigares,*
which sounds :
> see see see see see seegar
> see sah see see see see sah see seegar,
and means :
> 'If six saws saw six cigars
> six hundred six saws saw six hundred six cigars.'

Tongue-twister : *Un bon chasseur doit savoir chasser sans son chien* – to be said very rapidly. In English it is only, 'A good hunter should be able to hunt without his dog.'
Another : *Les chemises de l'archiduchesse sont-elles sèches ou archi-sèches?* 'Are the archduchesses blouses dry or arch-dry?' Can't get the effect in English.

Apropos of the expression *capiteux*, for wine which goes to your head, Monsieur Fissier quotes : *une blonde capiteuse,* or, *une brune capiteuse.*

*

19 June, Tuesday. Early morning at Lavail. The sound of the birds is something liquid, I sense the fluidity of movement in the sound and think that it is a transformation and refinement of the sounds a liquid substance can make – water perhaps. Water flows, falls, bubbles, boils, steams, evaporates. Somewhere in that flowing, falling, bubbling, boiling, steaming evaporation are sounds of motion and mixture, of soft turmoil, of descending and rising into envelopment and resurgence that the throat of the bird adapts, transforms.

Or am I wrong?

The sound of the bird is an adaptation of air, not liquid. The bird whistles in his throat, the liquid air flows through the soft throat of the bird, the throat chooses the sound of the flowing air, each sound one of the possibilities of the air, chosen, magnified, repeated. We sit in the early morning on a slope of the Pyrenees in a wood of cork-barked oaks and listen to this throat-whistling of the birds, this audible fluid : the repeated notes seem to ring, resound, softer, louder, lower, higher, rapid, repeated. At times I think they are sucking in the air, at others forcing it out. The sun shines sideways from the east through the oak trees, falls on the eastern sides of the trees in patches only where the thick growth of trees and foliage and bush allows it through. The cork-oaks are skinned as far up as the workers could reach and there the bark grows back smooth and brown, above that line it is grey and furrowed, cracked, a rugged texture of sun and light and shade and deep shadow. Everywhere the wood is this mixture of things, a complex pattern of darkness, deep shadow, shade, light and brightest sun falling in irregular patches, all mixed up, confused. But I do not see confusion. The irregular pattern pleases. The tiny green leaves of the bush that catch the sun are brighter yet, greener yet against the dark brown shaded bark of the cork-oak beyond. Everything contributes to this pattern : the trees, the grey rocks, themselves patterned with lichen, moss, irregularities, the fallen leaves, the heather, brush, grass, the occasional butterfly, the hovering mosquitoes, the swiftly moving flies, the intermittent, repeating sounds of the birds. To the south the mountains, peaceful, but to the north I can just hear the sound of early traffic, the distant roar of cars and, distant but coming closer, voices, boys calling, clamouring. Above my head the irregular pattern again, this time of branches and leaves against the sky. A dog barks. Insects sting. Ants crawl. Everything moves. The pattern changes, remains, persists, evolves.

And down below, back near the road, the sunlight reflects from the dust, shines in warm tones against the bottom of the lower branches of the cork-oak above it. A special kind of luminosity. And beyond, the brown of the new bark of the tree is warm and dark like wine.

At the café we have big cups of coffee without milk, because there is no milk, and bread and *confiture*. We wonder if there is no milk because she does not like to give out her own pure mountain milk to customers, but she confirms that the dark apricot jam is home-made, last year's produce. When we talk about the earliness of the hour she remarks that the clock is two hours ahead of the sun. She tells us that her daughter goes to work at six o'clock clock-time, that is, four o'clock sun-time, picking peaches. She herself gets up at two-thirty sun-time every morning. We discuss this theme for a while because it interests me too. She says many farmers have gone back to arranging their day according to sun-time. The other time is supposed to be a device to save energy. What good does it do? she asks. People sit around for hours watching television anyway.

The old lady comes out and stands near us and we chat. We ask her to sit down but she prefers to stand because she is just about to go in for her breakfast. But she stands and talks for a long time anyway, almost all about foods and plants, and when I look up I find her and Satia in a typical recipe conversation: 'Then I grind it up very fine, pulverize it very very fine in a mortar and pestle, and when it is very very fine, all ground up, I start to add the oil drop by drop . . .' accompanied by delicate, graphic gestures of pounding with mortar and pestle, adding oil drop by drop. I love these recurring recipe conversations. They reflect care and concern for the people who are going to eat the food.

On the way down we pass a group of young Dutch students gathering insects. They show us their prisoners in glass test-tubes closed with cotton, and seem proud. Cars pass, the air smells bad after them. Crossing the campsite we see that there is one camper, a family in a trailer with a tent raised against the side of it. In front of the whole thing is a huge televsion aerial held high in the air with guy-ropes.

*

The day after the *cargolade* Madame Fissier asks how I disgested.

'Well,' I say.

She remarks that her sister-in-law has just prepared seven hundred snails. She notices my surprise as she says this.

'For a big celebration?' I ask.

'No, for the freezer' – *la congélateur*. She casts her eyes downwards and reflects for a moment. Then : *voilà un bon approvisionnement d'indigestion* – 'A good stock of indigestion.'

*

We come back from our early morning walk to Lavail to find a strange car and two people about the Fissiers' age waiting for them. Friends, no doubt. But where are the Fissiers? They seldom leave so early. I invite the unknown couple in for a cup of coffee but they decline politely. We go off again and when we return about noon they are still there, that sadly disappointed, bored look intensified.

Where are the Fissiers? I rehearse the possibilities. They have not gone to Auchan, the hypermarket where they sometimes go early and stay for lunch, because they went there only a few days ago. They have not gone to Spain for shopping because they were there last week. They have not gone to Argeles because they would be back by now.

'The beach, perhaps, for a swim,' the friend suggests.

'That's out,' I tell him. 'They never go to the beach. They are almost always right here, at home. He loves to work around the house.'

Then it occurs to me : they must be at the doctor's, some doctor's. That is the only thing that could keep them away so long. And we invite the friends in to lunch, but they decline politely and disappear.

I sometimes think that Monsieur Fissier's illnesses are his grand amusement, that he enjoys having himself fiddled around with by doctors and surgeons. Then at other times I realize that they are genuine and he would love to find a true cure that would allow him to keep on working around house and garden.

It turns out that the Fissiers have been to the acupuncturist, which was a sad experience because they had to spend a lot of time with defective children who were also waiting for treatment. The incoherent movements and gestures of the mentally defective, their animal-like sounds and screams. The acupuncture was made in the children's heads and several people had to hold them. The scene made Madame Fissier very sad. Her life has been centred on the raising of her family, that was her most serious occupation and preoccupation, and she feels how the parents of defective children suffer. The talk turns to euthanasia and from euthanasia to the death penalty. Not far from here a little boy disappeared last month. Only two days ago his murderer – a seemingly normal neighbour – was discovered. Madame Fissier is firmly for the death penalty. She reflects on how many parents have been deprived of their children by murderers, madmen. Mental unbalance is no excuse, prison no guarantee against a repetition. Examples.

The Fissiers excuse themselves and go to bed early. They are fatigued and saddened by the day's experiences.

*

Satia, after shopping, reports that all the women of Argeles are talking of the death penalty – the guillotine – for the murderer.

*

Early morning meeting with André, after a walk to Lavail. He shakes hands, and then takes us over to the little stream that runs through his land near the house. He warns us that what he is showing us is secret – *parce qu'il est interdit – hein?* and takes a fish-trap out of the stream. It is all made of iron wire, a fine mesh of narrowing spaces. The fish can swim in but is unlikely to find his way out again. Inside, a fine big eel. *Déjeuner pour trois personnes, n'est-ce pas?* – lunch for three – and he adds that they will make the eel into a *bouillabaisse.* All the while he is smiling and laughing.

The hood of his old Deux-chevaux is up and I look inside. I have never seen one before and for a moment I wonder whether the motor has been removed. '*Où est le moteur,*' I ask, half jokingly. He shows me the two cylinders and we discuss the incredible reputation of the car : almost two-hundred thousand miles on one engine, and so on, and he shows us the long dip-stick in the gas tank that takes the place of the fuel gauge. 'You never put gas in,' he adds. Much laughter in general.

Then he shows us the tractor, nineteen years old. Again he laughs, and explains that he never once thought to change the oil in almost twenty years. Then the other day he couldn't shift gears so he took the gear box apart. There was no oil left. All he had to do was add oil.

While we are admiring the simplicity of the car he tells us there is something broken. It turns out to be the brake. He shows us where the hydraulic line is leaking out fluid. At times you are driving along and find you have no brake, he tells us. What do you do then? he asks himself, and us, and answers the question too, acting it out, making the sound with gritting teeth : You use the hand-brake. And he laughs. Hard to realize that his father was killed in a car crash not many years ago. André is the true farmer, he laughs about the difficulties.

When we discuss farming he also laughs, even though he is telling us about the disastrous decline in vineyard profits. Twenty years ago, he says, a hundred litres of wine brought the farmer a hundred francs and a farm worker's wage was also a hundred francs. Now a hundred litres of wine brings in a hundred and fifty francs but the wage has gone up to five hundred francs. Wine is not profitable.

*

Monsieur Fissier talks about going home for leave during the war and hearing the train repeating : *J't'amène, j't'amène* over and over;

going back to camp he heard it saying : *J't'ramène, j't'ramène.* When he repeats it it sounds like a train chugging, but the second phrase is heavier than the first, and he explains that the train was going downhill when he was on the way home, uphill on the way back.

He then tells the joke about the French prisoner of war who woke up and thought he heard a train, then realized that it was two German masons building a wall. As one handed up bricks to the other and the other took them they said : *Bitte schön, danke schön, bitte schön, danke schön,* and so on.

The GB on the British-registered cars stands for *Grosses Bêtes,* NL on the Dutch ones for *Nouvelle Lune.* The slang for 'police' is *vingt-deux* – 'twenty-two.'

*

24 June. More confusion in the post office. The blonde has got a holiday at last and two new girls have come in to take her place. They have no knowledge of the rules at all and so have to look up everything. And how complicated everything is! Satia goes to ask how much it will cost to send a book back to a friend in Trôo and is told, after much searching through pages of listed prices, that it will be six francs – 'book rate.' She wraps the book up and takes it back to the post office and is told it will cost twelve francs. There is no book rate for France, only for abroad. She shrugs her shoulders and pays.

Then come the books for Ireland. We have got so many books we can't get everything into the trunk of the car, so we want to send them home. But the postal strike is still on in Ireland. They won't accept anything – postal embargo. We decide to have the packages weighed up, wrap them, put on the correct value of stamps, and leave them thus ready to go with the Fissiers, who will mail them when the strike is over. There is also a package of clothing we don't need. We go to the PO with the package of clothes and the books in a big box, not packed, because we have to weigh them first: the maximum for books is five kilos at a time. The new girl weighs them up for us and we find we have less than ten kilos. We make two packages. There are some books left over so we have to

113

go home for more cardboard and string, and so on. But we hand over the first one for weighing and stamping. The girl sets the handles on the stamp machine and produces the correct postal-meter-machine-printed stamp. She puts it on the package. We take the package home. When we get back with the other packages she decides that we can't take them away once she has put the postal-meter-machine-stamp on them. Much consternation. 'What about this morning's package? Is it going to be necessary to buy some more stamps for it?'

She gives us that queer look. 'What do these foreigners want?' is what she is asking herself. 'Why do they want to mail packages and not mail them, all at once?' Ireland is such a little, insignificant place that she has not heard anything about the postal strike there. It is late afternoon and she has been catering to foreigners' demands all day, a long day of searching for figures, weighing things, seeking appropriate charts and running her long lacquered fingernail down columns of numbers to the correct one, multiplying weights by rates, dividing in half for 'book rate' (if it applies), getting confused, and so on and so on. Everything is too complicated, even the simplest of things. Nothing is simple.

*

Monsieur Fissier talks about his life: called into the French army three times, once before the war, then again when the war started, then after the liberation but before the war ended. In between he was on his parents' farm, where he got through in relative tranquillity because the Germans did not draft farmers into forced labour. Otherwise he would have been sent to Germany to work. Also, as a farmer he had enough to eat. Then, after the war, three factories. The first an iron foundry, the second bath-tubs, the third soap. Each time he got better pay. The third factory doubled his salary but he was under pressure all the time. His immediate superior did not like him, so no promotion. But he did well enough to buy his plot of land here and build the house.

In return, his illnesses: a long history of bronchitises, kidney-stones, torn Achilles-tendons, worn-out knees, and so on, time in hospitals, cures, long periods in bed. A heavy price paid for the work he forced himself to do.

'I did it for my children,' he concludes. 'Otherwise it would not be worth it. When you have children you need money,' and he rubs thumb and forefinger together.

For her part Madame Fissier confides that she is not very content here. She would rather be back home in Compiègne with her children, grandchildren, old friends. It is lonely here, in spite of good neighbours.

*

Themes of French life :
– the war – dead, suffering, occupation (but you no longer see the war-wounded, the mutilated – they have disappeared);
– work – the factory;
– the neighbours : conflict, cooperation;
– alcoholism;
– guns: *fusil, carabine,* accidental killings, *cambrioleurs* – burglars. Fissier talks of putting up a fence which no one may cross; he has the right to shoot anyone he finds on the inside of that fence; his conflict with the man across the way;
– the machines, the noise;
– *la voiture* – the car – the 'last freedom'.

*

Le Puy : Looking down from the Aiguilhe Saint-Michel, on one side red tile roofs, on the other stripes and checks of market gardens, the green of the growing vegetables, the dark purple-red of the earth. Slowly I realize that that earth is lava. Hundreds of little strips and squares below me, they are the private kitchen gardens, but across the main road a large field with many broad strips, vegetables and salads in all different stages of growth. An old couple, man and wife, are working, sowing seed in fine rows along a broad stripe of dark red lava. The rows are so fine and neatly drawn that from here they could have been made with a comb. He draws out a line with his hoe, she follows bending over, sowing the seed, and as she sows he goes back behind her and begins the next row. The stripe must be ten yards wide and over a hundred long but patiently they progress line by line, seed by seed, over the neatly raked ground. I can see what they have done today – five yards, perhaps, because in the section before that some green is already appearing, and more green in the section before that, and even more before that, and all done by hand on the finely raked ground. From the low grey clouds thunder sounds and lightning flashes, the rain begins, but they go on working. On another patch two men hoe cabbages, turning over the earth as they work and breaking it up. Giant pink ragged-robins grow from the steep rock just under where I am standing. I see them as I look down on the working couple. The rain is getting heavier so I turn as the drops fall on my notebook and climb up the winding stone steps past thistles and bluebells to take refuge in the porch of the chapel. At each point that the steps complete a circle I look down and see them working, drawing out lines and sowing seed.

*

Rue Portail d'Avignon, Le Puy :
LIBEREZ LES OBJECTEURS – A BAS TOUTES LES ARMEES
Free the conscientious objectors – down with all armies.

*

Hôtel Grand Cerf, Le Puy : a man in overalls eating lunch, then, later, dinner. He is young, well fed, with rosy, full cheeks, a black beard. As he eats, chewing his food vigorously, tilting his head, looking out of the sides of his eyes, he is like a Gustave Doré illustration to Rabelais.

*

An old woman making lace in front of her shop in Le Puy. She works the bobbins without looking at them. It is a form of braiding but with four threads. The bobbins pass rhythmically back and forth, she handles them with all her fingers busy and makes the work seem easy. We begin to talk. Other tourists stop and look. She asks them how they say *dentelle* in their language and from their answer she deduces that they are Dutch. Later she asks me as well, but when I say 'lace' she hesitates. There are too many possibilities, she is uncertain, so I tell her I am American. At once she talks about the wife of General Pershing, who came to buy lace from her in the nineteen-twenties. She went with the general's wife, in her chauffeured car, to look for another special piece of lace – *Elle m'a fait monter dans sa voiture, c'est un bon souvenir*. Then she adds: *Mon homme a fait la guerre de quatorze-dix-huit avec les américains*. I mention Pershing's 'Lafayette, we are here,' but she has never heard of it, never heard of Lafayette's trip to America.

She learned lace-making when she was six – seventy years ago. She considers it a craft that will not be revived. We get on to that theme. Hand-work is too slow, it does not pay well enough any more, therefore cannot continue. When she learned lace-making everyone was doing it.

But there is so much unemployment – *chômage* – it is the constant theme of the newspapers, and at the same time so much work not done – *travail qui n'est pas fait*. Here too it is hard to get people to do the work. She explains : it is too expensive employing people, there are all the extras to be paid, social security, various insurances, and so on. If she employs someone without registering the employment she is continually worried about an accident. If someone is hurt, who will pay the bills? And then there would certainly be an investigation, and a steep fine. Better to do without the help. But hence, also, there is unemployment. Too many social benefits impede progress.

She talks of her house, dated 1453. She does not tell me the date herself but refers me to a painted inscription on the café next door, which is part of the same building. A few years ago she had the roof re-done. She thinks the old roof was the original one. She would like to re-do the building itself but she thinks it is too far gone. The stones are too old. She regrets the thought of leaving because she loves the old lava-paved square where there is no traffic and children can play. 'See,' she says as a rubber ball bounces into sight and a boy runs after it, 'they play ball here.'

*

Le Puy. On a wall near the *Aiguilhe* :
DEHORS CE GOUVERNEMENT RACISTE ET ANTI-
OUVRIER – UNITÉ CONTRE LES EXPULSIONS
Down with this racist, anti-worker government – Unity against
the expulsions.
(Refers to the government's plan to encourage foreign workers to
return to their own countries.)

*

Vézelay. Our visit to the basilica suddenly shattered by the deafening
sound of the full organ, fortissimo jazz as it can only sound on a
huge church organ. We wonder what has got into the organist, but
it turns out that the basilica has been hired out for a wedding. The
young organist, a friend of the happy couple, is in to rehearse for the
afternoon ceremony. Friends gather round and try out the keys and
foot pedals of the organ while he himself enjoys various short blasts
of pieces half-remembered, half-forgotten. It is the full organ that he
enjoys most, a blasting noise. The young Franciscan friar who has
been lecturing school boys on the spiritual beauties of the basilica
stops to chat, turns a deaf ear to the ugliness of the noise.

The wedding itself is more restrained, a mixture of traditional,
folk and modern. The bride has dyed hair and a hard face, the bride-
groom looks bored. The friends who are in to make folk-music have
the best time.

When the noise of the wedding subsides at last in the late afternoon the only sounds are the footsteps of tourists who have come to
look. It is clear they have no religious interest in the place but their
quiet footsteps restore a sense of dignity, of contemplation, to the
atmosphere. It is only later, when the tourists too have cleared off
to look for supper that the empty building again takes on an element
of divine beauty. In the absence of worshippers it becomes a church
again.

*

Paris, café on the Rue Emile Zola, sun outside, inside I watch the
reflections of people passing in the polished marble and aluminium
sides of the bar. The surfaces are separate, reflect disparately, like a

distorting mirror in facets, and I watch little trunkless pygmies walk into it, their heads on their waists, wait for the traffic light to change, walk on out of the scene.

*

Champ de Mars. The shade of the long avenue of plane trees. The sun is bright, even in Paris, but here it is shade with only flickers of soft light on the dust of the unpaved walk. They are pruning the trees. There a tall ladder, extended to fifteen yards, against one of the plane trees. The breeze is chilly in spite of the sun. Four men stand holding long heavy bamboo poles with hooked pruning saws at their ends; other saws are in large holsters at their sides like sheathed swords. They hold their bamboo poles erect like long and powerful spears. They are resting, regaining strength before more work, before the next ascent. A pigeon flies away from a tree nearby. The men stand and look upwards towards the trees, point, discuss, stand and rest, their saws at their sides, their long poles held still, erect. One of them rests his bamboo pole against the tree he is going to prune, goes back to where he has left the long extension ladder, carefully raises the top of the ladder from its point of contact with the tree, leaning gently backward, pulling the ladder upward, away, towards himself, takes hold of the rope, thus freeing the upper extension and folding it downwards into the lower section. He pauses, rests, then shifts the ladder's weight on to his shoulder, the ladder itself at just the right angle, just rightly tilted away from the vertical to distribute its weight correctly, and carries it to the tree he is going to prune. Once more he takes hold of the rope, pulling it to him. The extension rises, slides between branches, rises to its full length. He climbs. He reaches the top but does not stop. Thirty feet up he climbs off the ladder on to the branch. Out on the rocking branch, outward. The branch sways, rocks. He goes fifteen feet from the trunk and finds a natural seat, a place to straddle the branch and also have a back-rest, the junction of three parts. Though he is wearing a thick safety rope around his waist he does not bother to hook himself to the tree by it. Instead he turns the bamboo pole which he has carried with him from the ground into position and starts to saw at branches another fifteen feet further away. He prunes the next tree too. His own branch rocks and sways but he continues sawing away at it. Finished, he climbs back along the branch, back to the trunk, on to the ladder, down to the ground. He drapes the safety rope around his neck and begins sawing at the branches he can reach from the ground with the long pole. The other three stand and chat.

Métro portraits.

The nose first, the straight nose, the perfectly descending sides of perfectly vertical nose, flanked by the two round wings, dark holes of nostrils, the perfect symmetry, composed form. Then the impression of light hair, short, combed around the face, itself straight, like the nose, and the descending sides of the face almost vertical, perfect symmetry and composition. The mouth matches the eyes : both full, almost large, horizontal, symmetrical, balanced. The perfect form, the balance, give a sense of containment, reserve, but the largeness of the eyes and mouth suggests strength, fullness of the self, a potential, a capacity. All connected by the straight nose: determination. Surrounded by the trimmed blond hair, casual but neat: softness.

.

His face is long, long and the chin is pointed, and his brown hair is long too, and though it is straight it waves to follow the curves of his head and neck. Little freckles on the tan skin, and dark brown eyes like a cow's eyes – empty of thought, restlessly moving right left seeing not noticing, young man's unformed eyes, the full dark semi-circles of cow-eyed Juno. The long nose, thin at the top, bulging, swelling irregularly outward downward to the downturned nostrils. The mouth a crescent inverted, corners down. The pointed chin comes forward. The mouth chews, chews gum, without opening. Devoid of meaning, fixed thought. A young man's face, face of future potential, perhaps. The quality of perhaps. Perhaps in a face.

.

Chewing gum, chewing gum, with big mouth-opening chews, jaw muscles expanding, contracting, pulling, tightening, chewing gum, head slack, light summer dress and light sandals, left leg over right, nylons, white summer jacket, tan leather bag, peroxide hair, slack body, chewing gum, waiting, no thought, chewing gum.

．

Round, tight, compact, bulging, a face that has seen work, much work, the eyes resigned, the nose bulging, modestly, the lips closed, thin, withdrawn into the mouth, the slight gold-rimmed eye-glasses, the plain brown hair, neat, modest. Has she spent so much time caring for old people? The sick? Only the chin protrudes, a little knob of determination. Over the print dress she wears a tan knitted cardigan. One hand is on the suitcase resting beside her in the aisle. Disappointment of the past, leading to resignation. The self second, the self third, the self last.

．

What was this face like when it was younger? The fatigue of long life. The lips are tightly closed to contain the indignation. But they were full, they were soft. That softness is denied now. Behind the lightly tinted glasses the eyes are sad, the white hair is thinning. Her nose is large and long. But she sits erect, held erect by respectability, respectability and endured sadness, thought, thinking of things past, family, children, events beyond control to suffer or resist because events to others. Her sadness is not for herself, it is for others. She continues, hopes, sits erect, her overcoat tan and clean and neat here in the Métro. Only, under the sadness, a little bit of animal brightness survives, the face of one who was active, always active, every day.

．

This heavy head that is half hidden behind the large dark glasses. The clipped hair adds to the effect of sculpted wood. Is it a woman's head? Head and arm and legs are like a man's, and the large set mouth and the thick lips are bitter. There is a set of bitterness to the mouth, and even in the way she sits.

*

As the taxi came on the pigeons scattered. One was too late. The wheels barely grazed him but something happened. At first I thought his tumbling and flapping, rolling over and half flying an inch above the road was his confused hurried way of getting back to the pavement, safety, where other pigeons pecked. He was flopping his escape wildly to the side of the road, wings flapping, feathers escaping, and rolled thus into the stream of water that the street cleaner had turned on to flow fully along the gutter, cleaning it, rolled over on his back there and settled with a few quick adjusting movements of wings and legs into repose. I was steps away when he met the taxi but he is already in this composition of repose when I stop to look at him, dark slate head and neck and tail, light grey body, underside of wings a pearly white, claws the colour of *vin rosé*, or of old much-polished red leather. The water subsides from the gutter as the street cleaner diverts it in another direction and the dead pigeon lies on his back in his unwilled repose.

*

7 a.m. *Parc Montsouris.*
7.10. Métro, *Cité Universitaire.*
7.12. Train.
Zombie people, still in their sleep, though awake; few read, most just sit, some with eyes closed. I see their faces as I would see them when they sleep. They are still trying to recover the dream, the night's experience. Reluctantly they have forced themselves awake to go to work, work which is not them, they are something else, elsewhere. Where?

The emergence at Châtelet, the vast hall of tiles and mirrors, its multiple symmetries, so that no orientation is possible apart from the commanding, instructing signs. A barrier of stainless steel: used tickets in, out they come again, take them between fingers, sign flashes the go-ahead, walk through the barrier, the guard stands and watches, without movement, without word.

The moving carpets, moving at walking pace; we walk on and walk along, others on the one going in the opposite direction also walk, and we walkers pass other walkers not at normal walking pace but at four times normal walking speed. We seem to glide past our fleeting encounter away.

The constant in Paris is the drone, which is always there, becoming a whine and then a roar when you come close enough to it, the roar and whine of vehicles, constantly there, constantly.

Two workmen preparing to repave the little area around a water-spigot in the Tuileries. The mixing of the sand and the cement, the mixing of the mixture with the water, the tearing out of the old cobbles, the setting up of the line, taking measurements.

The Métro again: the faces that have forgotten how to smile, the downturned corners of the mouth, the inverted crescent that is the lips, faces that cannot smile, faces of despair, and fear. It is the fear that this is true, and that this will go on being true, that day after day the Métro will be his fate, he will not escape the Métro, day after day, every day.

*

A visit to the Sainte Chapelle to hear a concert. We had forgotten that the Sainte Chapelle is enveloped by the Palace of Justice, which covers the whole city block. At the gates of the high black fence that closes the Palace of Justice off from the street we ask a policeman about the concert and he directs us to a long flight of wide steps on the other side of the courtyard. On our way to them we can just see, over the walls of one of the inner wings of the justice building, the very tops of the tall Gothic windows of the chapel, and the delicate high spire. We join a crowd that mills around on the steps. There is no real line, everything seems to be in disorder. A large group of American students arrives, their pink concert tickets in their hands. Finally the doors open and two policemen come out

and start calling for ticket-holders. The students and others who have
the pink tickets push through the crowd, which hardly makes way
for them. Repeated calls from the policemen for ticket-holders and
those who have invitations. More holders of pink tickets push through
the crowd along with some urgent-looking people who hold white
slips in their hands.

While we are waiting I notice that a large police van has slipped
into the courtyard and pulled up near one of the doors. A group of
policemen are escorting a young woman to the van, one of them
holding her firmly by the arm. She is not very cheerful, her walk
tells of her discomfort. Suddenly I realize that there is a jail not far
off, or some kind of place of detention. The young woman is put
inside the van, and a few policemen get in too, but others stand
around outside it. It does not drive off but stands, and I stand,
looking at it, thinking of the prisoner inside, sensing only very
slightly by sympathetic resonance the unpleasant sensation of being
a prisoner, being held against your will on a hot, clammy night of
the Paris summer.

Ticket- and invitation-holders having pushed through, the rest of
us are finally let in. More police on the inside. We buy our tickets.
Still more police as we move along the corridors. They are the ushers.
Slowly we shuffle our dishevelled way towards the Sainte Chapelle.
We really are a messy lot, some of us have not even bothered to
shave, none of us are well dressed. It is hot and muggy, the air is
polluted with a greasy kind of car exhaust, there is scaffolding in
front of and around us, and we are shuffling along under the stern,
unyielding eyes of the Paris police. As we shuffle into the scaffolding-
clad porch of the Sainte Chapelle we get a quick view of the archi-
tectural situation : we are going to hear a concert of ancient music
in an ancient Gothic chapel, but the Gothic chapel itself has been
built into the massive police barracks of central Paris. It is an odd
sensation.

Did I once admire the architecture and beauty of the Sainte
Chapelle? I cannot quite recollect, especially now when it seems
to have been turned into a hall with rows of grey plastic chairs and
a large vertical tunnel of composition board running up the wall
in front of one of the windows. Microphones on long arms criss-
cross our view of the apse. The gawdy dark wall-paint is chipped

and unkempt, as shabby, almost, as we are – we, the crowd. Taking it all in, I wonder why the neat, clean police tolerate us.

Then the concert begins – the programme, but not the music. We are called to attention and a speech begins, blaringly amplified, blasting into our ears from the loudspeakers only feet away. The Paris summer festival (*festival estival de Paris*) is being advertised. A long speech. We grow restless, applaud. The speech goes on. Then we get some recorded music from the loudspeakers. *Recorded* music? What's going on? Then more speech-making. More restlessness, more applause, and so on. Then at last the musicians, six Englishmen in dark trousers and white shirts without ties, take their places at the music stands, open their mouths, sing. I know this is ancient church music I am hearing, but what is wrong? Can it possibly have been so strident and harsh? But it didn't sound that way at Winchester Cathedral when the choir was singing evensong. It didn't sound that way at Solesmes Abbey when the monks were chanting vespers. Are these young men overdoing their lung muscles? Or are the loudspeakers still on? Loudspeakers in the Sainte Chapelle?

After a while we give up. Music was not meant to hurt the eardrums. With relief we slip past the policemen at the door, the policemen in the corridor, the policemen at the gate. Around the corner a large group of policemen stand in a doorway, looking impatient. One of them eyes us fixedly and we move off hastily. Around the next corner more policemen. A police-car issues from a gate at high speed, blue rooflight flashing, quickly followed by a truck-like police-wagon. They roar away up the street and out of sight. We decide not to bother with the concerts at the Sainte Chapelle.

*

Going to 'down-town' Paris – Boulevard Saint Michel – to look at books. The feeling of suffocation in the closed, windowless, artificial-light bookshops. Many people, hot atmosphere. Back to the Luxembourg Gardens, a walk around. A band-concert about to begin. I sit down on one side of a two-sided bench, three Venetians sit on the opposite side, talking. I listen with pleasure to the soft tones of their dialect and catch the words 'American band'. So it is an American band about to give the concert. Another American band. Where do they all come from? How do they get the money to be all over Europe giving free concerts? Mystery.

They start some kind of jazz piece – disappointingly for me, but – relief! – break it off again after ten or twelve bars. A white-haired conductor comes up to replace the younger man who was conducting. I look at the band now and see that it is a youth band, they are all about thirteen or fourteen, some possibly younger. And this is evidently a kind of public rehearsal. I wish them well.

They begin again. This time it sounds – improbability! – like something Russian. Only an imitation, no doubt, of the harmonies and rhythms of Shostakovitch. They play for a minute or two, then things start going wrong with the trumpets. Another pause. Silence. Discussion. Finally they begin again, get through the whole piece. Applause.

I begin to wonder whether this is a concert or a rehearsal. From the proceedings I conclude that it is the latter. I look at the band from where I sit on my bench beyond the circle of green chairs around the bandstand. They are all dressed in black, they look very young. But then a woman comes around handing out mimeographed sheets. It turns out to be 'The American College Band'. College? I go up to the bandstand to have a closer look. Sure enough, they could be in college. I look some more, walk around the stand to make certain. Yes, they could be in college, and I am surely getting old to take them for teenagers, but still there is something wonderfully embryonic about them, a quality of emptiness that I don't get elsewhere, something it would be hard to imitate, if anyone wanted to. They simply look as if there was nothing there.

I walk on through the Luxembourg Gardens, soaking up the retreating roar of 'God Bless America', and come to a dust field where groups of men are playing *pétanque* – rolling metal balls ever so delicately to get them as close as possible to a little wooden ball they have thrown out first, or hurling their metal balls at full force to push away an adversary ball that got too close. A fascinating game of skill where slight rises and falls in the pebbly ground can make a world of difference. Concentration, back-spins on the ball, pride, disgust.

The players are mediocre today, so on to FNAC, the huge three-storey bookshop on the Rue de Rennes. This is even worse than the ones on the Boulevard Saint Michel, even more airless, even more crowded, even more given to artificial light. I leave almost as soon as I go in. A young woman outside wants to ask me three questions – 'only three questions' – about racism. I stop.

First question : am I a racist?

I say 'Yes, I am.'

Taken aback by this, she puts a quick check in the appropriate column of her notebook. Out of about twenty checks already on the page I am the only one in that column.

Second question : do I object to interracial marriage?

'According to circumstances,' I say. Another check in the wrong column.

Last question : do I know about the treatment immigrant workers receive in this country? The question answers itself, so she doesn't wait for my answer. Instead she tells me about the cause for which she is collecting money, a publicity centre in Paris to plead the case of immigrant workers. I am a bit indignant about the roundabout manner she has chosen to get money out of me but I put my hand in my pocket.

'Will you give me twenty francs?' she asks.

'I will give you a franc,' I say. To me it seems like a good rate of return for a moment's conversation, and I pull out my hand with some coins. She looks sour, asks again for twenty francs, sees my refusal, points to a two-franc coin and asks for it.

'Give me that coin.'

I give her a franc. She takes it, disparagingly. I look at her and she reads my look.

'All right,' she says, 'thank you. At least it's something.'

Back to the Luxembourg Gardens by the quietest side-street I can find. Just as I get near the bandstand the band is finishing its concert. I hear the closing bars of 'Stars and Stripes Forever'. The crowd gets up and starts to move off. My only concern is whether a lot of them are going to make for the 38 bus, which I am planning to take home. But just as I reach the gate a 38 pulls up at the red light, and

I rush ahead to the stop and am there to get on, and get a seat, when the bus arrives at the stop. We get away before the crowd.

*

At the last moment we decide to go to the Sunday matinée at the Comédie Française. They always keep ninety-five tickets for sale at the last minute, at eleven francs each. The tickets go on sale half an hour before the performance. We get there at 2 o'clock, just before the window opens, and get on the end of the line. At once we notice people arriving after us but trying to sidle in ahead of us. Instead of shoving we decide to give way. '*Après vous, Madame,*' I say to one old white-haired lady I see, '*je vous en prie*', and I hold my hands out to indicate the place in front of us. The old lady, who is evidently only trying to establish who is last so that she can get on at the end of the line, does not notice the sarcasm of my tone. Instead she accepts the place, expresses her surprise at being so courteously addressed, declares that we cannot possibly be French, for the French have given up being courteous, no longer use terms of address like *Madame, Monsieur*, and so on. In fact, she confesses, she is ashamed – *j'ai honte* – of being French, so badly have manners deteriorated.

And Paris is so dangerous. Seven years ago, just before her retirement, she was going home from work on the Métro in a fierce crowd, so dense you could hardly move, when she felt a knife put to her throat (she illustrates graphically, her finger becoming the knife, held in under her chin and tight against her throat). 'Don't make a sound or I will kill you,' she heard. As it was the end of the month she had just received her month's wages – she worked all her life, she interpolates, as clerk, typist, then secretary – which she had in her handbag and which she needed badly, for at that time she was supporting her old and disabled mother. A most disheartening experience, she tells us. Then, looking at Satia, 'Never take the Métro. Take the bus. The bus is alright, but avoid the Métro.'

She likes to talk and we enjoy listening, so she goes on. The treatment of the old is abominable now in France in all respects, she says. She herself was evicted from her old apartment in Paris and forced to take a far more expensive one on the outskirts. Her old apartment had no shower or bath or central heating, but for that reason it was cheap, five hundred francs a month. Then she was evicted, on the grounds that they wanted to put in bath and heating, and had to move out of town to a newer apartment that cost one thousand five hundred a month.

Rapidly she explains the economics of her pension – too rapidly for me to follow everything precisely. Roughly : the rent takes most of it, a few hundred francs left over for gas and electric and heat, and finally she has about ten francs a day for food and other daily expenses. Hardly enough. So she is moving to Brittany, to a little island off the coast where there are no cars and life is cheap.

'Only,' she adds sadly, 'there is no Comédie Française. It is not Paris.'

The line is moving now and we try to keep moving with it, which interrupts the conversation. She asks where we are from.

'Americans,' I say.

Ah, she remembers how the Americans gave them bread when they were hungry after the war. And now it takes America to send them someone with manners.

She buys her ticket just ahead of us and when we get up to the first balcony we find we are sitting next to her, right on the very side of the theatre. She is talking to a white-haired man who is about her own age, discussing the theatre. The play is Molière's *Misanthrope*, and it is given the full classic and traditional treatment. She whispers her admiration of the sets – *un tableau de Velasquez!* – to her friend and in one of the pauses between the acts I hear her telling him she was born too late, much too late – *beaucoup trop tard* – she really belonged in the eighteenth century. She could not approve of the modern world. Which, of course, is just what Molière's misanthrope keeps saying about his own time. And every time he delivers another verbal slash against the men of his time the old lady nods enthusiastic approval, so appropriate to our own time is the criticism he makes of his.

When the play is over and we get up to go she extends her hand and thanks me again for having made way for her on the line – *de m'avoir cédé votre tour*. Will she see us at *Ruy Blas*? she asks. She recommends it highly. She will not be going to *Dom Juan*. It is a modern production, the sets almost bare. She prefers the classic style.

*

Paris is colossal, monumental – itself a monument, a colossus striding its Seine. It is smaller in extent than London or New York, than many cities, but its construction is bigness. It is the great 'I' of cities.

What was it like before they cut the broad boulevards that lead the view down long avenues of sight? Before they tore down the many little bee-hives of neighbourhoods to make those long boulevards possible? Built the huge monuments of architecture that dwarf our merely human selves when we visit them? Was it too human, that city of people? Did it encourage them to think that their city was for them and not for the impersonal necessities of imperial greatness? If so, the rest of us know nothing about such motives, for we obediently visit the great monuments, do homage to their builders, their royal patrons.

But I find no way to put myself in the picture – to *myself,* that is. The broad, straight boulevards seem custom-made for modern traffic, as I walk along the sidewalks I am conscious of nothing but the roar and fumes of many cars. That is what I hear, breathe. It is the true life of Paris. From time to time as I walk I come to a place where the broad road broadens out still wider, a great round place where the walker must make a large detour, describe a semi-circle to continue his walk. Here three or four avenues cross, a vast star with six or eight radiating entries and exits is formed. Not only do I find myself making an unwilling deviation to get back on my original route but at every crossing I must stop and wait for the mechanical permission of the traffic-lights. Permission given, a quick rush to the next stage of waiting, and so on until the walk resumes at last in the original direction. That is the experience of the walker in Paris.

Sunday morning, after a visit to Notre-Dame, we find ourselves sauntering along the Rue Sainte Geneviève, into the Rue de la Montagne. There is little traffic, since it is Sunday, and the streets are small, irregular. It is warm and windows are open and from one house, from a large open window not far above the street, we hear the sound of a grand piano pouring its chords and melodies through the open window. We stop and listen. It is real music, not recorded music amplified, and we listen to this bit of genuineness with appreciation. It is neither mechanical nor monumental nor impersonal : it is human, real.

We continue on along the Rue de la Montagne until we come to a little square, the very top of the Rue Descartes where it meets the Rue de l'Ecole. Here the buildings are still old, old and narrowly rising their five or six storeys. Obviously they would fall, would be unable to stand were they not crushed in thus shoulder to shoulder, like spectators at a football match, each one holding up his neighbours and held up by them. Perhaps – who knows? – inwardly fainting, falling, but now unbudging nevertheless by reason of the mutual buttress of the party-wall. It is the symbol of the city, its life. They are still in use and serviceable. One is even a hotel, with a single white-on-blue star issued to it by the Tourist Board.

So we curve on round past more small hotels, small restaurants, narrow houses, past the church of Saint-Étienne-du-Mont, until we arrive at the Panthéon. Splendid name! *Panthéon.* The gods of ancient Greece are dead but their words live on in the gods of France. Vaguely I recognize that it is a recreation of something ancient : its architecture is taken from the building of the ancients, but how vast, how enormous! It is so high and wide I can hardly see it. It is so big that I lose all sense that it was meant to mean anything. It says, *I am big.*

Inside, it seems yet bigger. Are those figures at the end people? How tiny they seem in these huge spaces, beside these high pillars! How insignificant. It is true, we must be in the presence of gods, some kind of gods, even if only the gods of monumentality. The message : if the architecture of the ancients was good, we will make it even better – by *multiplication,* by *enlargement.*

Later I visit UNESCO and when I leave I turn to walk along the Avenue de Saxe. I come to the perfect circle of the vast Place de Breteuil. Its ideal geometry is wasted on me, however, for all I see before me is another problem in pedestrian navigation. The white lines painted on the road make it plain that I am expected to take the wide semi-circular path around, not cut directly through the middle. That second, shorter course is in any event dubious, hazardous, because of the traffic rushing into the circle from eight separate directions. If the way is clear at any given moment it may not be for long. I begin a clockwise circumnavigation but stop in the middle of the first intersecting avenue, the Avenue de Breteuil. A game of *pétanque* is in progress. The central stripe of the avenue is planted with plane trees and left unpaved – expressly, I wonder, for the sake of the players of *pétanque*? I stop to watch the game. The ground is rough and gravelly, full of irregularities, little holes, stones that are always getting in the way, deflecting the carefully aimed metal balls. The players are from anywhere but Paris – most of them – you can tell from their faces, their stance, their voices. Italy, Spain, Provence. They play with pride, aim with care, calculate their shots, brush away irregularities with their feet, measure the doubtful ones with tapes, discuss, shrug shoulders, exult briefly and quietly in victory. The game and its players hold my attention.

Between two games I look up, look along the Avenue de Breteuil, and with a quick astonishment I perceive a beautiful small chapel, a chapel of perfect proportions, a jewel. Human-size, a pleasing adaptation – at last – of classic forms : delicate columns, a graceful rising dome. My eyes are fixed on this chapel, I do not look away, for in the moment of this unexpected experience my mind is rapidly reviewing the topography of the city, calculating places, wondering how I could have overlooked this perfect small gem of construction, the only thing I have seen in Paris that can be taken in with a single look, that does not demand a tiresome series of pacings, cranings, peerings up and down, side to side, followed by the intellectual process of reconstructing in the mind the inspiration and purpose of the builder. It is an experience like the many I have had in the provinces, a church built for its users, for people.

My enjoyment of the sight is marred by my own mind, my own curiosity. It is not enough to look, I must also know what it is, what it is called, where it is, why I have not seen it before. I fish in my jacket pocket for my street map of Paris, unfold it, turn it over, seek out the proper locale, locate the Place de Breteuil, the Avenue de Breteuil, establish my position, rotate the map into correct orientation, look along the delineated avenue, find the church.

I am looking at the Invalides, the Eglise du Dôme of the Invalides. Now my astonishment is even greater, for I have often passed that church. What? That tasteless pile of stone, as overwhelming and unapproachable by its size as any of the monuments of Paris, as the Panthéon itself?!

Quickly I see what has happened. It is the most baroque of deceptions, the most successful I have ever experienced. I had thought I was near to a chapel of perfect size and proportions, of perfect beauty, but it is the *perspective* of the avenue that has deceived my eye, my senses. The church is half a mile from me. If I walk towards it, approach it and see it as I usually do, it will crumble again into a disunited assembly of its parts, into a colossus, a monument, a church not to God but to the king.

I look again at the players of *pétanque*. Exclamations, shouted counsels, exultations, shrugs. The ground is rough, the course of the metal ball is uncertain, unpredictable. They do not seem to play as well as their counterparts in the provinces, in Collioure, Beaucaire, Arles. It is hard to concentrate here for the air is dense with car fumes, the noise of traffic is loud and distracting.